W9-CAV-330

Praise for *Unprotected*

"This is a punch-in-the-gut powerhouse of a book by a very brave clinician. The message is provocative and profound. . . . I wish others had the guts to speak out in a similar fashion." —Cal Colarusso, M.D. Training and Supervising Analyst, San Diego Psychoanalytic Institute

"A household name here at Hopkins psychiatry as the best contemporary example of a good doctor who notices what is happening around her and to her patients and strives to do something about it." —Paul McHugh, chairman of psychiatry at Johns Hopkins University

ABOUT THE AUTHOR

Miriam Grossman, M.D., has been a psychiatrist at UCLA Student Psychological Services for more than ten years and has worked with students for twenty years. She received her BA from Bryn Mawr College, her medical degree from New York University, and her psychiatric training through Cornell University Medical College. She is board certified in child, adolescent, and adult psychiatry and is Senior Fellow at the Clare Booth Luce Policy Institute. Dr. Grossman lives in Los Angeles with her family.

The author can be contacted through her Web site www.MiriamGrossmanMD.com

UNPROTECTED

A CAMPUS PSYCHIATRIST REVEALS HOW
POLITICAL CORRECTNESS IN HER PROFESSION
ENDANGERS EVERY STUDENT

MIRIAM GROSSMAN, M.D.

Previously published under
the name Anonymous, M.D.

SENTINEL

To my children,

Tanya, Shuki, and Chasida,

whom I have always tried so hard to protect

SENTINEL

Published by the Penguin Group

Penguin Group (USA) Inc., 375 Hudson Street, New York, New York 10014, U.S.A.

Penguin Group (Canada), 90 Eglinton Avenue East, Suite 700, Toronto, Ontario, Canada M4P 2Y3
(a division of Pearson Penguin Canada Inc.)

Penguin Books Ltd, 80 Strand, London WC2R 0RL, England

Penguin Ireland, 25 St Stephen's Green, Dublin 2, Ireland (a division of Penguin Books Ltd)

Penguin Group (Australia), 250 Camberwell Road, Camberwell, Victoria 3124, Australia
(a division of Pearson Australia Group Pty Ltd)

Penguin Books India Pvt Ltd, 11 Community Centre, Panchsheel Park, New Delhi – 110 017, India

Penguin Group (NZ), 67 Apollo Drive, Rosedale, North Shore 0745, Auckland, New Zealand
(a division of Pearson New Zealand Ltd.)

Penguin Books (South Africa) (Pty) Ltd, 24 Sturdee Avenue,
Rosebank, Johannesburg 2196, South Africa

Penguin Books Ltd, Registered Offices:
80 Strand, London WC2R 0RL, England

First published in the United States of America by Sentinel,
a member of Penguin Group (USA) Inc. 2006
This paperback edition with a new preface published 2007

10 9 8 7 6 5 4 3 2 1   1 3 5 7 9 10 8 6 4 2   1 2 3 4 5 6 7 8 9 10

Chapter Four of this book was published, in part, on worldnetdaily.com.

Grateful acknowledgment is made for permission to reprint excerpts from
Creating a Life by Sylvia Ann Hewlett. Copyright © 2003 Sylvia Ann Hewlett.
Reprinted by permission of Miramax Books. All rights reserved.

THE LIBRARY OF CONGRESS HAS CATALOGED THE HARDCOVER EDITION AS FOLLOWS:
Unprotected : a campus psychiatrist reveals how political correctness in her
profession endangers every student / Miriam Grossman, M.D.
        p.   cm.
Includes bibliographical references (p. 153).
ISBN 1-59523-025-4 (hc.)
ISBN 978-1-59523-045-4 (pbk.)
1. College students—Mental health.
        RC451.4.S7U5   2006
616.8900835—dc22   2006044355

Printed in the United States of America

AUTHOR'S NOTE

———

To my patients, whose stories I have told: I take seriously my responsibility to respect your confidentiality, and I have taken great care to do so. All names are fictitious, and other characteristics and circumstances have been changed to protect patients' identities. I have tried not to include any information that might in any way identify you. Any resemblance of the disguised identities I used in this book to any actual person is entirely coincidental.

To my readers: I have tried to thoroughly research these subjects, and have ventured into fields not my own. I may have inadvertently made an incorrect assessment, for which I take full responsibility. Please remember that this is not a definitive medical textbook, but the experience of a campus psychiatrist.

Finally, I regret the necessity of quoting vulgar material and describing offensive subjects. I knew of no other way to support my claims.

CONTENTS

PREFACE

———

WHEN THIS BOOK WAS INITIALLY PUBLISHED, IT DID NOT HAVE my name on it. The title was *Unprotected: A Campus Psychiatrist Reveals How Political Correctness in Her Profession Endangers Every Student,* by Anonymous, M.D.

A year earlier, I had made this decision with considerable ambivalence. As a new author, I was unaware that publicity began early; I still had months of research and writing to do when I learned that in a few weeks, Sentinel's catalog would appear. There would be my name, on a book that challenged the dogma of my profession. What, so soon? I asked. I'm not ready!

I was worried about the response to *Unprotected*: our campuses and mental health organizations do not always celebrate ideological diversity. But I needed to focus on completing the manuscript—no easy task. Distraction, worry, and what-ifs would only stand in my way.

Sentinel's suggestion, "Anonymous, M.D.," didn't sit so well with me either. I was proud of my work and had nothing to hide. So I went back and forth, with neither option feeling quite right.

In those early days, I was isolated, depending on moral support from family and friends, one colleague, my agent, and my editor. Sometimes it didn't feel like sufficient backup, considering I was indicting practically the entire field of health and counseling . . . did I have that much chutzpah?

There were other reasons I hesitated. For example, there was the explicit material that I wouldn't want my own kids to see. Was I really writing a book that includes the word "condom" dozens of times? When I began the project, I'd cringe imagining *Unprotected* in the hands of a particular relative or my rabbi. If I'm lucky, I thought, they'll never hear about this.

There was no such luck, and now I'm grateful for that. Less than a week after publication, Dr. Laura "outed" me. It was with my permission, of course. By that time I had some significant figures behind me: Nick Cummings, Ph.D., an ex-president of the American Psychological Association; Cal Collarusso, M.D., an eminent psychoanalyst and educator; and Joseph McIlhaney, M.D., who had been on the Presidential Advisory Council on HIV/AIDS and founded the highly respected Medical Institute for Sexual Health. These doctors were acknowledged experts and the authors of many scholarly books and articles. After reading the entire manuscript, each of them had endorsed my work with fervor. I was no longer alone.

Dr. Laura's promotion was unbelievable. She read three pages from my introduction on her show, and said, "I'd like to sit here and read the whole book to you. . . . Finally, somebody has the giblets to stand up. . . . On a scale of one to ten, this book is a twelve." I'll never forget how it felt to hear those words.

And that was only the beginning. Then came excellent reviews in the *Wall Street Journal*, *National Review*, the *American Spectator*, the *Weekly Standard*, and elsewhere. Fox News and *Newsweek* booked me, and I flew out to Pat Robertson's 700 Club. I was interviewed on over one hundred radio shows and spoke at the Family Research Council, the Best Friends Foundation, and the Claire Booth Luce Foundation in Washington, D.C.

Best of all were the letters and e-mail. They poured in from young men and women, parents, grandparents, psychologists, teachers, nurses, physicians. The gist of their message: Your book should be mandatory reading for every college student. I'm going to send it to every young person I care about. Thank you for your courage.

In the midst of all this recognition was a remarkable thing—a *lack* of response from those I had challenged: the American College Health Association, the American Psychological and Psychiatric associations, Planned Parenthood, Columbia University, and others. No corrections or disagreement. No attempt to set me straight with the facts. No attention to the book whatsoever.

Sure, there were individual colleagues who took my attack personally, and were livid. "How could you do this?" one of them asked, apparently too hurt to recognize I was addressing issues that were larger than the two of us, our center, and our campus. But there was no official response.

Maybe it's too early to expect reactions from large organizations and institutions, or maybe they think if they ignore me, I'll go away.

Well, that's not going to happen. You see, I'm a woman with a mission, and one of my goals is the large-scale revision of sexual health education. This will require the excision of ideological agendas and close scrutiny of how we use a number of terms, including "safe," "risk," and "protection."

With that in mind, I want to issue a challenge. I am calling for Columbia University to explain its promotion of high-risk behavior on their site GoAskAlice.com. I want to understand how, in the face of national pandemics of herpes and HPV, these "health experts" can advise a high school senior, who has already had three boyfriends, to continue to "experiment," and "explore" her sexuality, claiming that doing so will "only add to [her] future well-being and peace of mind." Exactly what study, I'd like to know, has demonstrated that? And to the freshman who is wondering whether to lose her virginity to a boy she's known only three weeks, "Alice" says: "three days, three weeks, three months, three years? There is no right time to have your first intercourse. . . ." Are parents aware, I wonder, of the "guidance" their daughters will find on this award-winning health education Web site of one of the most esteemed institutions in the world?

I am troubled that an authority like Columbia University gives the green light to casual sexual encounters. Early sexual debut and multiple partners are well-established risk factors for cervical cancer and infertility. If the priority here is health, isn't this precisely the behavior we need to discourage? Alice's advice is at best irresponsible, and at worst perilous. I suggest she take a more thoughtful and cautious approach:

> *Thank you for writing in with your relationship question. The fact that you've made this effort shows that you're not certain about the best course of action.*
>
> *Your gut feeling tells you this is a big decision, and that is entirely correct. The consequences of sexual behavior—whether "protected" or not—can be profound. There can be long-term effects, physical and emotional, that reach far into your future. Also, this is a very personal matter. I wonder if perhaps you are without an older and wiser person in your life, and that's why you have turned to this site for guidance. Sometimes when a young person lacks a close and trusting relationship with an adult, they turn to sexual behavior, thinking it will satisfy that yearning. This may or may not be true for you, but it's worth thinking about.*

This response might encourage a young person to think twice before "hooking up" and placing themselves at risk for STDs, unwanted pregnancy, and emotional turmoil. But in this upside down world, "Alice" is deemed "pro-women," whereas I am accused—by some readers—of spewing "right-wing drivel" and "anti-female garbage."

What's alarming as well is the lack of response to "Alice" from the many professional organizations whose mission is to promote the health and well being of young people. Where is their outrage? Or perhaps their silence indicates agreement?

I look forward to hearing what Columbia University has to say, and to a national debate on these issues that is long overdue. In the meantime, it's with deep satisfaction that a paperback edition of *Unprotected* is being released—with my name on the cover.

And by the way, in case you're wondering: that relative I was worried about and my rabbi? Well, they read the book, every word, and—can you imagine?—they're beaming with pride.

Miriam Grossman, M.D.
September 2007

INTRODUCTION

IT'S MONDAY MORNING, AND MY NINE AND NINE-THIRTY ARE both waiting. Before seeing them, I quickly check my messages, and learn that it's been a busy weekend: a law student made a suicide attempt; a women's studies major, who last week came out to her parents as a lesbian, fell down the stairs while partying and suffered a concussion; and the blood test I ordered on the freshman with bulimia showed low potassium—a condition due to vomiting that can cause an arrhythmia.

A busy weekend, but not an unusual one. Like everyone's at the campus counseling center, my schedule is overbooked, packed with appointments made by distressed students. Why the surge of bright, accomplished young people, students at one of the nation's best-known universities, flooding the offices of psychologists, psychiatrists, and social workers? They are looking for relief—from their crying jags, sleepless nights, relentless worrying, and thoughts of death.

Campus counseling centers are busier than ever. In a 2005 survey, 90 percent of these centers revealed an increase in the number of students seen with serious psychological problems. The number of psychiatric consultation hours doubled. Ninety-one percent of centers hospitalized a student for psychological reasons, and over 36 percent experienced one or more suicides.[1]

Why are our kids in such bad shape? People are all scratching their heads, and you've probably heard the speculation: Is it the stress of leaving home and adjusting to independence? Is it issues related to identity, sexuality, relationships, and roommates? Don't forget academic demands, parental expectations, financial pressures, and a competitive job market. How about the effect of 9/11? One academic has another angle. He points out, "today's college students distrust the nation's leaders. They have little confidence in the nation's social institutions. They see large-scale problems all around them."[2]

There's no doubt that these elements, and others, contribute to varying degrees. But I believe another factor, one you *haven't* heard, demands our attention. I contend that radical social ideologies are also to blame, especially when they've spread from the classroom to the counseling center. I once assumed campus medicine and psychology had one priority: student well-being. I'm no longer so naive.

Radical politics pervades my profession, and common sense has vanished. Not long ago, a psychiatrist might call casual sexual activity "mindless" and "empty."[3] Before political correctness muzzled our nation in the nineties, a campus physician might advise a student that it is love and lifelong fidelity that bring joy and liberated sensuality, and provide the best insurance against sexually transmitted diseases.[4] An unwanted pregnancy, an abortion—these were weighty issues. We understood that men and women are profoundly different, and weren't afraid to say so. It was clear that liaisons outside a committed relationship could be hazardous, and a young woman would be wise to wait until someone serious came along. A sexually transmitted infection, even one easily cured, was a serious matter. Self restraint built character, and character was something to strive for. Certain behaviors were abnormal, and those who practiced them needed help. Traditional marriage and parenthood were valued milestones. To search for meaning, and to make sacrifices for a higher purpose—these were noble endeavors that defined our humanity.

Things have changed. Now young people are advised to use latex, and have a limited number of partners (as opposed to unlimited?). There is tacit approval of promiscuity and experimentation: one study of college students speaks of "primary and casual sex partners."[5] Infection with one of the sexually transmitted viruses is a rite of passage; it comes with the territory. Abortion is the removal of unwanted tissue, sort of like a tonsillectomy. Campus counselors urge students to get enough sleep, eat right, exercise, and make time for themselves. Clubs funded by student fees celebrate risky, fringe behaviors.[6] Young women think motherhood can be delayed indefinitely; women's health teaches them only about *preventing* pregnancy. Traditional marriage and a mother and father are just one option; there are other alternatives, all equally valid.

These changes are the result of social agendas foisted on the campus community, and in my work at the counseling center, I see the consequences daily. Dangerous behaviors are a personal choice; judgments are prohibited—they might offend. Students have gender-free "partners": what difference does it make whether male or female? Attendance at a "multiculturalism" workshop—to increase my sensitivity and inclusivity, and confront my sexism, racism, and homophobia—is mandatory. When lesbians have a child, it's time to celebrate, but when Catholics or Mormons have their sixth, that's, well, kind of extreme, and the eyes roll. Staff are encouraged to attend a meeting featuring a transgendered person and his therapist, who describes the journey from female to male. The mental health benefits of church attendance are never discussed; instead, a past president of the American Psychological Association (APA) declares organized religions a major source of social injustice. A committee of that organization is worried about what I think and how I speak. They advise me to never assume that a patient is heterosexual, or that sexual activity might lead to pregnancy. I should avoid thinking of men and women as "opposites," as in "opposite sex." I should not use this term, the committee cautions, "to avoid polarization."[7]

My profession has been hijacked.

I cannot do my job, my patients are suffering, and I am fed up.

Unprotected tells the stories of college students who are casualties of the radical activism in my profession. These were students who turned to me for help in the midst of a crisis. They often wept, and sometimes, unknown to them, I wept with them. Their dramas were disturbing and unforgettable.

Despite using "protection," Stacey had HPV, a sexually transmitted infection. Campus health focuses on "safer sex," so I had no tools to encourage behavior change.

Would she soon have herpes? Amanda will likely miss out on motherhood, because the "women's health" program on campus focuses on contraception, not future families, and she's probably waited too long. Can I treat her insomnia? Brian has anonymous encounters with men in the university community, but HIV testing is "a personal decision," and judgments are prohibited. Will his life, and that of others, be cut short? Heather thinks women are like men, so she's puzzled when her "friend with benefits"—a man with whom she has a physical relationship, no strings attached—is content, while *she* hates herself. Is Zoloft the answer?

My patients were hurting, they looked to me, and what could I do? Unlike other physicians, my hands were tied. Cardiologists hound patients about fatty diets and insufficient exercise. Pediatricians encourage healthy snacks, helmets, and discussion of drugs and alcohol. Everyone condemns smoking and tanning beds. Aren't health-care professionals supposed to address their patients' lifestyles?

Apparently not. I see many patients who endanger their health—sometimes their lives—through high-risk behavior. But I'm just supposed to say, "Make sure you're protected." Protected? Who am I kidding? Stacey thought she was protected, and so did Heather—now they're paying the price.

Where I work, we're stuck on certain issues, yet neglect others. We ask about childhood abuse, but not last week's hookups. We want to know how many cigarettes and coffees she has each day, but not how many abortions are in her past. We consider the stress caused by parental expectations and rising tuition, but neglect the anguish of herpes, the hazards of promiscuity, and the looming fertility issues for women who always put career first. We strive to combat suicide, but shun discussion of God and ultimate meaning.

Inaccurate and ideology-driven "health education" misinforms our sons and daughters, increasing their vulnerability. HIV is presented as an equal-opportunity infection. Despite substantial failure rates, condoms are endlessly enshrined. Young women are led to believe that, like men, they can delay childbearing indefinitely. The emotional consequences of STDs and abortion are downplayed. A popular Ivy League Web site includes tips on behaviors that were classified as mental disorders in the eighties, the pre-PC era when I was trained. But as of 1994, sexual sadism and masochism are considered disorders by the APA only if they cause a person distress or impairment. Ten years later, following this controversial decision, this Web site was recognized for its "outstanding contribution to the profession of health education through technology."[8]

Being fed up and angry, I wrote *Unprotected*. I would have preferred to steer clear of these topics, but this book came and pounded on my door. It entered my life, chapter by chapter, with the students who walked into my office. Meeting Brian, Amanda, Sophia, and the others forced me to examine the radicalism in my profession, and propelled me to speak out. But it also brought fear and worries. What price will I pay for being politically incorrect?

You probably didn't know what some insider psychologists are now revealing: that "psychology, psychiatry, and social work has been captured by an ultraliberal agenda" and that there are "special interest mafias" in our national organizations. Likely you didn't hear that certain points of view are "squelched,"[9] that there are "horror stories" of "shunning and intimidation," and that many will not speak up, fearing ridicule, vicious attack, or loss of tenure or stature. A past president of the APA, in a book about this alarming situation, wrote, "I lived through the McCarthy era and the Hollywood witchhunts and, as abominable as these were, there was not the insidious sense of intellectual intimidation that currently exists under political correctness."[10]

Perhaps due to a measure of intimidation, perhaps just wishing to avoid conflict, at work I kept my views to myself; you might say I was "in the closet." Many coworkers were zealous about the changes they wished to see in society—I knew they worked tirelessly, in and out of the office, to promote causes they considered right and just. This dedication defined their lives. I feared, if I dared speak up, labels and strained relationships. Perhaps they would stop referring patients. Who knew what could happen? So I stayed clear of controversy; when e-mails or comments bothered me, I let it go.

Yes, the university, and my department, were committed to the principles of diversity and multiculturalism. This commitment was plastered all over our policy statements. But somehow, through the years, I got the sense that the diversity that *I* represented wasn't the same type to which they were so profoundly commited.

Furthermore, the ideology of the staff was the ideology of the university. My beliefs might come to the attention of people in powerful positions. I was but one person, of low rank, and I'd be drawing attention to myself, attention I didn't want. As long as I could do my job and take care of students, it did not appear to be prudent, appropriate, or even relevant to publicize my beliefs.

But then I met Stacey and Brian, and I had a problem: how could I *not* speak up? Their stories were not unique— they were undoubtedly being told by young people all over the country. There are seventeen million students enrolled in our nation's colleges and universities.[11] Many are still adolescents, impressionable and confused; they are at a critical point in their development, questioning who they are and what they want. Others have biological illnesses: bipolar disorder, schizophrenia, obsessive-compulsive disorder. For help, students turn in hordes to their campus health and counseling centers. I see firsthand how the politicization of these centers is hazardous and wrong. Hazardous, because our kids are deprived of facts they need to make informed decisions, while risky behaviors are sanctioned. Wrong, because it is unethical to promote a particular social agenda while providing medical or mental health services.

As a parent, I know that behind most students are a mother and father who are worried, hoping, praying for their child. I want to warn them: in addition to binge drinking and date rape, there is another danger on campus that warrants your attention. You probably assume that if your child needs to visit the student health or counseling center—a "free" service, after payment of mandatory fees and insurance—the physician or therapist will be a neutral agent, providing objective information and guidance. Think again. The nurse teaching your daughter about herpes, the social worker reassuring your son about his homosexual thoughts—these people may have a vision for social change that you don't share. They may see their jobs as an avenue for activism, and one of their goals is to influence your child.

The social change some of them envision is profound. They hope to destabilize a truth of science and civilization: that the sexes are deeply and essentially different. Their goal is an androgynous culture, where the differences between male and female are discounted or denied, and the bond between them robbed of singularity. I contend that to turn the therapy session or clinic visit into an instrument promoting this agenda is a corruption of the health profession. It demands a response. It's bad enough that androgyny, promiscuity, and "alternative sexualities" are promoted by Hollywood; it is altogether another matter to have them endorsed by professional health organizations and college administrators.

These agendas are promoted by devoted professionals who are motivated by altruism. Nonetheless, damage is done. Students in treatment are endangered, as the prevailing anything-goes attitudes are officially endorsed, rather than challenged. And like secondhand smoke, the behavior of one can affect many, as these students interact, influence, and "hookup" with their peers. As we ponder the epidemic of depression, cutting, suicidal behavior, and eating disorders on our campuses, I suggest we look first in our own backyard.

It bears repeating that it is my fellow professionals I fault here, not the young people we all strive to help, and that these are health, not moral, issues. I argue as a scientist, with biological facts, not biblical ones. Forget Leviticus—as you'll see, my data is from *The New England Journal of Medicine* and the Centers for Disease Control and Prevention.

My argument is simple. If someone's my patient, I'm responsible for her—*all of her*. Who says I should worry about alcoholic binges but not hookups? What, her liver's more important than her cervix or fallopian tubes? I'm going to discourage certain behaviors, my colleagues will say? You bet I am! The real question is: *how can I not?*

So I* am speaking out, because I have to. But the story isn't finished. Even as I write these words, months before publication, I'm still "in the closet" at work: still not "out" with my values and beliefs. It's my choice; I'm just not ready. How odd, that among people who know so well the pain of hiding, I must hide. How sad, that in the midst of those flying the banner of tolerance and multiculturalism, I should hesitate. How scandalous, that the very profession we trust to guide and heal is sowing confusion and illness.

---

*The identity of Dr. Miriam Grossman was revealed on November 20, 2006, on the *Dr. Laura Show*.

CHAPTER 1

Unprotected

HEATHER WAS A NINETEEN-YEAR-OLD STUDYING PERFORMING arts. She came in during her freshman year to see a psychologist, due to moodiness and crying spells that came out of nowhere. Normally upbeat and social, Heather was always ready for a good time. But in the past months, she had often withdrawn to her room, feeling worthless—even self-hate. These episodes were painful, and had started to interfere with school and friendships. She tried eating better and practicing yoga, but Heather couldn't get back to herself, and she didn't know why. The psychologist sent her over to me.

As we spoke, she stressed that her moods really didn't make sense, because life was good, and there was nothing to complain about. Heather liked school and had many friends. Her family was supportive. She had enough money. Her health was fine.

"How long has this been going on?" I asked.

"Oh, I don't know. Maybe . . . I guess since the new year. I've always had low self-esteem, but now it's really bad."

"Did anything happen to you around that time?"

She thought about it. "No, I don't think so. . . . I can't think of anything."

There are times when symptoms may appear without any precipitant, but I decided to ask again. "Heather, please think about it carefully. In the fall or early winter, did you lose someone you love, or have a pet die? Did you go through something frightening or dangerous? Did any relationship begin or end?"

She thought it over. "Well, I can think of one thing: since Thanksgiving, I've had a 'friend with benefits.' And actually I'm kind of confused about that."

"Really? Tell me more."

"Well, I met him at a party, and I really like him, but there's this problem. I want to spend more time with him, and do stuff like go shopping or see a movie. That would make it a friendship for me. But he says no, because if we do those things, then in his opinion we'd have a *relationship*— and that's more than he wants. And I'm confused, because it seems like I don't get the 'friend' part, but he still gets the 'benefits.' "

She was genuinely puzzled. She had no clue whatsoever.

"I think many people would feel the way you do," I told her. "You're giving what he wants, but not getting what you want."

"Yes," she agreed. "I'm really unhappy about that. It's hard to be with him and then go home and be alone."

We talked about her frustration and her wish that things were different. "Do you think," I ventured, "that these moods you have, when you are so unhappy and critical of yourself—do you think they may be related to this?"

She considered my question. "I don't know ... maybe.... What do you think?"

Olivia, eighteen, is also a freshman. She was valedictorian of her senior class, and hopes to go to med school. But Olivia just told me that she's been vomiting up to six times a day, so I'm sending her to the lab right away, to get her blood drawn. If her potassium is low, it could cause an abnormal heart rhythm.

Olivia originally developed bulimia in the ninth grade. With therapy, she did well, and she thought that the bouts of binging and vomiting were over, until she got to college. It's not the academic pressure—she is doing well in all her classes. No, it was the end of a romance that precipitated the relapse and brought Olivia to our center for help. Her therapist recognized Olivia's depression and eating disorder, and referred her to me for evaluation. During our initial meeting, Olivia described the short-lived relationship, her first experience with intimacy. "When it ended, it hurt so much," she said, weeping. "I think about him all the time, and I haven't been going to one of my classes, because he'll be there, and I can't handle seeing him. I was so unprepared for this.... Why, Doctor," she asked, "why do they tell you how to protect your body—from herpes and pregnancy—but they don't tell you what it does to your *heart*?"

Olivia was a smart girl asking a good question. Why are students inundated with information about contraception, a healthy diet, sleep hygiene, coping with stress and pressure—but not a word about the havoc that casual sex plays on young women's emotions? It's not as if there isn't any research on the subject.

For those who trust academic journals more than Mom's wisdom, take a look at some recent research. In a study of 6,500 adolescents,[1] sexually active teenage girls were more than three times more likely to be depressed, and nearly three times as likely to have had a suicide attempt, than girls who were not sexually active. Another report, titled "You Don't Bring Me Anything but Down: Adolescent Romance and Depression,"[2] analyzed data on 8,000 teens. The two researchers concluded that "females experience a larger increase in depression than males in response to romantic involvement," and "females' greater vulnerability to romantic involvement may explain the higher rates of depression in female teens."[3]

So the professors agree with Olivia: a broken heart hurts. And most likely Olivia's heart hurts more than the heart of the guy who dumped her. "Females' greater vulnerability"— that sounds right to me.

Sure, there are women on campus who are making wise choices in their relationships. But if you think Heather and Olivia are unusual, I have news for you: our schedules are overbooked with them. They're lining up for appointments and flooding our phone lines. I've seen so many students like these, they blur together in my mind, a pitiable crowd of confused, vulnerable young women, ill prepared for campus life, making poor choices, and paying high prices.

No amount of Prozac or Zoloft is going to solve this problem. These young women must, for their physical and emotional well-being, change their lifestyle. And the therapists, doctors, and nurses they consult have a responsibility to encourage them to eliminate their emotionally destructive behaviors, much as they would instruct an obese or nicotine-addicted patient to diet, exercise, and stop smoking.

Is it feasible? To acknowledge the negative consequences of the anything-goes, hooking-up culture would challenge the notion that women are just like men, and undermine the premise of "safer sex." And in our ultra-secular campuses, no belief comes so close as these to being sacred.

How are women like Heather and Olivia educated to make healthy choices in their private lives? What guidance do they get from university resources, like health and counseling centers, Web sites, and newspapers? Would parents—who fund these resources through taxes and student fees—approve of their content?

I set out to answer these questions after hearing the stories of Heather and Olivia—stories that were without a doubt being repeated innumerable times on campuses all over the country.

Soon I had a pile of brochures and Web sites to study. One thing was certain: there was no lack of information about the importance of diet, exercise, and sleep. A "healthy lifestyle" also includes learning how to relax and cope with stress. And obviously smoking is out. In fact, the American College Health Association went so far as to publish a position statement on tobacco on college and university campuses, which declares that "tobacco use in any form, active and passive, is a significant health hazard" and encourages colleges and universities to be "diligent in their efforts to achieve a campus-wide tobacco/smoke-free environment."[4] To this end, the ACHA recommended a number of actions, including: prohibiting smoking in all public areas on campus and in all campus housing (including lounges, hallways, stairwells, elevators, restrooms, and laundry rooms), offering prevention and education initiatives that address the risks and support nonuse of tobacco, offer programs that include practical steps to quit using tobacco, prohibit the advertising or sale of tobacco products on campus, and prohibit the sponsorship of campus events by tobacco-promoting organizations.

This is all good and fine—I agree that smoking is a nasty habit. But I was looking for something that would address the emotional distress of my patients. For example, to help Heather and Olivia understand their very normal reactions to relationships, and to guide young women to make healthy decisions, I was looking for material that declares casual sex hazardous to a woman's mental health. That aside from distress and anger, it can cause symptoms that will interfere with her ability to concentrate and perform academically. That hours better spent in the library will be used crying with girlfriends and at the campus counseling center. That her GPA—that mighty figure, critical to grad school acceptance—may fall. Such material could include data from the studies mentioned above, showing that girls are more vulnerable to depression when it comes to romance. It could also mention the fascinating research on the biochemistry of bonding.[5]

Neuroscientists have discovered that specific brain cells and chemicals are involved in attachment. The chemical Heather and Olivia need to know about is called oxytocin. It's a hormone, a messenger from one organ to another, with specific tasks; in this case, it's sent from the brain to the uterus and breasts, to induce labor and let down milk. Not a surprise, then, that oxytocin is also involved with maternal attachment: a female rat injected with it will bond and protect another female's young as if they were her own.

More relevant to my patients at this stage in their lives is that oxytocin is released during sexual activity.[6] Could it be that the same chemical that flows through a woman's veins as she nurses her infant, promoting a powerful and selfless devotion, is found in college women "hooking up" with men whose *last* intention is to bond?

Here's how one neuropsychologist put it: "You first meet him and he's passable. The second time you go out with him, he's OK. The third time you go out with him, you have sex. And from that point on you can't imagine what life would be like without him. . . . What's behind it? It could be oxytocin."[7]

The release of oxytocin can be "classically conditioned" —after a while, all it takes for it to be released is catching sight of the man. Is Olivia avoiding class because seeing him will bring a surge of this hormone, a rush of agonizing feelings of attachment?[8]

In addition to bonding, oxytocin increases trust.[9] Researchers studying financial transactions made this remarkable discovery when they had pairs of subjects play a game in which they risked real monetary loss. Each was given a whiff of either oxytocin or placebo, then they played a game in which investors could win or lose based on their partner's honor or betrayal. Those who inhaled oxytocin had more trust in their partners; they took risks avoided by the others.

You might say that we are designed to bond. Neuro-endocrinology is suggesting that, in their unfortunate liaisons, Heather and Olivia unknowingly promoted powerful feelings of attachment and trust. Thus Heather's yearning, and Olivia's melancholy, may have roots in their biology.

Information members of our hooking-up culture, indoctrinated to believe they are "protected" by latex, need to know? I would think so. So why haven't they heard of it? Why isn't oxytocin—likened to a "love potion" by one neuroscientist[10]—part of the vocabulary of our youth; why aren't they as familiar with it as they are with carbs and fats, nicotine and steroids?

I submit that the notion of being designed to bond is to some an unwelcome finding. It implies that sexual activity, especially in women, might be more complex than, say, working out. It suggests women may be vulnerable, unprotected. To some on campus, these are fighting words. Psychology is strongly biased towards liberal views;[11] do the actions of oxytocin threaten the feminist agenda? I can think of no other explanation for the failure of this research to make headlines.

"When research is swept under the rug," read an article in the American Psychological Association's *APA Monitor*, "some of the best psychological research suffers for the sake of 'political correctness.' "[12] This is the largest professional organization of psychologists in the world, and to their credit, here was an admission of the hazards of unpopular research: lack of funding, overcritical reviews, and labeling of researchers. For example, when his study showed negative consequences from day care, an author was called "sexist." Others reporting controversial findings were stifled by threats of legal action.[13] Maybe this explains why my patients, usually well-informed, are ignorant here: funding and publicity go toward research whose results support the politically correct agenda.[14] Women more vulnerable than men? You can't get less politically incorrect than that.

Has research about the biochemistry of bonding been swept under the rug? It seemed that way where I work and on the Web sites of other colleges I explored.

When I advised Heather and Olivia to refrain, for the time being, from having relations, I would have liked to hand them a brochure, or recommend a support group. And it would've been great if there was a policy statement from a major medical or women's organization acknowledging the legitimacy of my efforts, and encouraging campus officials to give their prompt attention to these critical health issues.

I didn't find what I was looking for. Instead, throughout all the material directed at teens and young adults, the mantra of "sexual rights" and "safer sex" was repeated ad nauseam. There were descriptions of every type of possible behavior, too graphic for my taste, and much attention to topics of which I'd prefer to remain ignorant.

Take, for example, the popular site goaskalice.com— a "health question and answer internet service" produced by Columbia University's Health Education Program.[15] Their mission: to provide readers with "reliable, accessible information and *a range of thoughtful perspectives,* so that they can make *responsible decisions regarding their health and well-being"* (emphasis mine). Parents with college-bound children, I suggest you take a look at this site, which gets two thousand questions a week, and many more hits.

"Phone sex—getting started"; "Health risks of bestiality": these are some of the topics up for discussion here. Just click on your mouse—you will find useful information about sadomasochism, "tools and toys," and drinking urine. To a question about a ménage à trois, "Alice" (identified on the site as "a team of Columbia University health educators, health care providers, and other health professionals") advises, "Nothing wrong with giving it a try, as long as you're all practicing safer sex." To a reader calling himself "will try anything once," Alice provides advice on proper "swing club etiquette," as well as a link to the National Swing Club Directory. And for a reader who's wondering "how to clean a leather cat o'nine tails between uses, especially if it drew blood," Alice can help: hydrogen peroxide.

You'll be tempted to think the unexpected topics found on goaskalice.com reflect the funky scene in Manhattan. Far from it. In my research of college Web sites, I found normalization of behaviors that were once considered illicit—if not perverted—all over the country. At Virginia Commonwealth University, cross-dressing is a "recreational activity."[16] At the University of Missouri, "external water sports" is described as a type of "safer sex."[17] (For the puzzled, a definition is provided: "urinating on skin without open sores." Still don't get it? This type of perversion was once called masochism.) Compared to that, the University of Wisconsin's tips for your *daughter* on how to pick up "that cute girl you noticed in your English class"[18] is tame.

No, there was nothing here that would help Heather or Olivia. No questions and answers about oxytocin, bonding, trust, and neurobiology. No consideration of the emotional consequences for young women of "hooking up." No data on their "increased vulnerability to romantic involvement." No mention of the truckloads of antidepressants prescribed to keep some of them functioning. No concern about campus counseling centers bursting at the seams trying to treat them all.

Why do the legions of Heathers and Olivias on our campuses not exist for "Alice"? Why her neglect of these victims of our culture? Why instead is she busy normalizing sadomasochism and other disorders?

Clearly, Alice's priorities—and those of many others with the responsibility of providing college students with "health education"—have nothing to do with addressing the problems of my clientele. My guess is that, like everywhere else on campus, Alice advises students from a place where ideology reigns supreme. Central is the dogma that desires are "needs," to be acted upon and satisfied; that behaviors considered aberrant by society and medicine are natural, while self-restraint is not; that regular sexual behavior—with or without a committed relationship—is necessary and healthy; and that any and all these activities can be free of consequences, as long as they're "protected."

But believing doesn't make it so. In the world I inhabit, there are plenty of consequences. On my campus, sexually active students are much more likely to seek counseling, and to rate their relationships as stressful. Almost daily, I prescribe medication to help students, mostly women, cope with loss and heartbreak. Like it or not, hard science suggests that intimacy initiates a trusting bond. Ask Heather and Olivia, two girls woefully unprotected: there is no condom for the heart.[19]

CHAPTER II

Damage Control

Stacey, twenty-one, was referred because she cut herself—not all the time, but following some stressful event, like a fight with her coach or roommate. More specifically, she would use scissors, a knife, or a razor to cut her forearm, not deep enough to hit an artery—she didn't want to die—but enough to see blood. We call it SIB—self-injurious behavior—and there's loads of it on campus. Most girls say they do it for relief from overwhelming emotions. Stacey, a French major, described it as "cathartic."

I listened with interest as Stacey shared her life with me. She was an athlete, a swimmer who had been recruited. She got up at five to do laps, and worked out at the gym for at least two hours in the afternoon. Her physical condition was a priority, and she was careful about what she ate. A vegetarian, she avoided processed foods and additives, and took lots of nutritional supplements. No alcohol, nicotine, or marijuana. No soda for Stacey—only bottled water. This wasn't easy with her demanding schedule, living on campus where most students grab a taco or pizza slice for lunch. But she had strong convictions about the benefits of this lifestyle, and felt the extra effort was worthwhile. Her body mass index, low blood pressure, and stellar performance in the pool were a source of pride.

Her family was "intact": her biological parents were married to each other and lived together. They had always been around and responsible, but unavailable emotionally. Her mother was on Paxil. There was one sibling, a younger brother with drug and alcohol addiction. Stacey was the star, the "together" one, and expectations for her were high.

The cutting began freshman year. She swam poorly at an important competition, and her coach was disappointed. Finals were coming, and the deadline approached for a research paper. There was a squabble with her roommate. Calling home for support, Stacey learned that Shawn had relapsed, was using again, and had totaled Dad's car. She didn't want to add to her parents' distress—compared to her brother's problems, hers were minor. That evening, angry and overwhelmed, she scraped a plastic knife against her wrist, and discovered a calming effect. Since then, it's a technique she has turned to again and again.

Prior to the referral for a psychiatric evaluation, Stacey had been seen for a year at our center, and made progress in therapy. Her social worker helped her to recognize the source of her emotional pain, to think, write, and speak about it. She gained insight and developed coping skills. Then there was bad news that put her over the edge.

Following her annual exam at Student Health, Stacey got a call from the nurse. Her Pap test was abnormal; she probably had a sexually transmitted infection called HPV. She needed to see a gynecologist, who might want to do a biopsy.

"I'm still so shocked," she told me. "When they first said I had it, I'm like, Oh my God—I've only been with a few guys, and they always used a condom. . . . I can't believe this is happening to me! I know it's the most common STD; they told me that there are a million new cases every year, and that usually it's harmless. But a few types of HPV are dangerous, they can even cause cancer! What if that's the kind I have? And the guys I've been with—should I tell them? The nurse said it's up to me. And should I tell my parents?"

She was in crisis, afraid and confused. It's true that most cases of HPV seem to be harmless and disappear, but at the same time, the virus causes nearly every case of cervical cancer. About four thousand women a year die in this country from cervical cancer, around the same number that succumb to AIDS. Even if Stacey was infected with a "low-risk" type, it could still cause warts on her genitalia and cervix, and the treatment of these warts[1] may be painful, cause scarring, and be expensive. The virus could be with her for life; there is no cure.[2] She could also transmit HPV to her newborn, causing respiratory disease. And being infected with one STD, she may be more vulnerable to others. I asked about her relationships with men. She'd been with four people, three in the past year. She used condoms every time. Stacey didn't always ask about STDs—it was too awkward, and anyway she practiced "safer sex." Or at least, she thought she did.

So here was a bright, self-disciplined young woman. She got up before dawn to swim thirty laps. She said no to cigarettes, pot, and alcohol. She didn't eat meat. She avoided people who smoke. Stacey's life was about self-restraint, self-control, and self-sacrifice in the name of a healthy body. Except when it came to her sexuality.

Having three partners in the past year increased her risk of getting HPV by three hundred percent.[3] The condoms her partners used didn't prevent its transmission.[4] The latex decreased, but did not eliminate, the risk of getting one of the twenty-five STDs that infect millions of her peers.[5] These bacteria and viruses cause genital blisters and ulcers, bloody and foul-smelling discharges. First, they are painful and gross. Then they can cause infertility, cancer, and death.

Student health services work feverishly to prevent sexually transmitted infections, and yet in one study[6] 43 percent of college coeds going in for their yearly exam get the same shock as Stacey: Your Pap smear is abnormal, you have HPV, it can cause warts, and rarely cancer. Why is it—with "safe sex" education starting in some places in sixth grade, and condoms available free at many student health centers— why is it that so many young women have HPV?

I submit that part of the problem may come from within the field of reproductive health. This discipline has been permeated by an ideology promoting permissiveness and experimentation; in order to preserve that ideology, the bar has been lowered. Instead of aiming for disease *prevention,* as is done in the fight against heart disease or obesity, the goal is risk *reduction*—aka "safer sex"—followed, when it fails to be safe enough, by *damage control.* Instead of the grim facts, women are fed oversimplified and whitewashed information. And when "safer sex" fails, the consequences— both physical and emotional—are minimized.

The American College Health Association tells Heather,

Olivia, and Stacey that they can have "safer sex": "Safer sex doesn't mean eliminating sex from your life. It does mean being smart and staying healthy. It means self-respect and respect for your partner—talking about sex, knowing how to protect yourself, and taking precautions every time. Safer sex means enjoying sex without giving or getting sexually transmitted diseases."[7]

How does a woman practice "safer sex"? She limits her partners, uses condoms, and gets tested regularly. Let's examine each portion of this advice, as it relates to HPV.

Limiting partners seems to makes sense: fewer partners means less exposure. But what does "limit" mean? Less than three? less than ten? less than your sorority sisters? And what if you limit your partners to one or two, but each of *them* has had ten? You've exposed yourself to ten, twenty people. And anyway, when a woman meets someone and likes him, she often hopes—sometimes subconsciously— that he *will* be the one, that it *will* become serious and last. So having that hope, she can convince herself that she *is* "limiting" her partners. How can she know in advance that it won't work, over and over?

HPV is so common and so contagious, especially in the college population, that most young women are infected within a few years of becoming sexually active, from one of their first few partners.[8] An expert in HPV advises college women, "You'd be wise to simply assume your partner has HPV infection."[9] In the past six months, I had two patients who were infected by their first partner, and one of these women had been sexually active on only one occasion. That's right: one man, one time . . . HPV. So much for the first item on the list of instructions for "safer sex."

Condoms: they're highly effective with some other STDs, but may not make a difference with this one.[10] Like herpes, HPV lives on skin that may not be covered by latex.[11] The infection is usually not visible and does not cause symptoms.[12] She doesn't know if she has it, and he doesn't know if he has it.

Even if condoms do protect somewhat against HPV, there's another problem with them: in spite of aggressive information campaigns and easy availability on most campuses, they're not used often enough.[13] The most recent study of heterosexual college students showed that less than half had used a condom during their last vaginal[14] intercourse, and that was an all-time high. The reasons? There wasn't one available, there was no concern about pregnancy, the participants were high or drunk, they considered themselves uninfected, it felt better. In one study, 41 percent of women said that a sexual partner had tried to dissuade them from using one.[15] When students do use condoms, they often make mistakes.[16] Breakage and slippage are frequently reported. Inconsistent use of condoms hasn't changed despite our massive efforts to improve education, skill, and availability. Nonetheless, most "safer sex" pamphlets for young people still sing their praises.

In December 2000, President Clinton signed Public Law 106-544, which directed the CDC to educate the public about HPV. Evidently, their efforts didn't reach Stacey.

Fortunately, she knew the importance of yearly gynecological exams. Unless Stacey had warts that were visible or bothersome, evidence of HPV infection was detectable only through a Pap test. Do Pap tests always pick up problems? Is she correct in assuming that, since this was her first test to be abnormal, she got HPV this year?

It's more complicated than that. One or more of Stacey's previous Paps could have been false negatives—meaning changes were present but not detected.[17] There are several reasons this could have happened, including human error. Reading a PAP smear involves scanning hundreds of thousands of cells for what could be a few abnormal ones. The specimen may have been poor, the lab could have been negligent. One hospital had a class action suit filed against it by women alleging "improprieties" with Pap smear testing procedures.[18] Some of these women have cervical cancer.

Yes, Stacey could have had HPV for years, ever since she became sexually active, and not known. Does it matter? Depends how you look at it. If she has a type that "just" causes warts, the only downside is that probably she unknowingly shared it with others. But if Stacey is infected with an HPV type that can cause cancer, there is a possibility that the time interval did make some difference, although most authorities agree it almost always takes years for disease to develop. Of course, "almost always" doesn't mean there aren't rare cases of women having invasive disease within a few years of their first abnormal Pap.[19]

There are other areas of uncertainty and debate. How long will Stacey be infectious? One pamphlet she might be given at the health center states: "The great majority of people eliminate the virus spontaneously. For others, however, as with most infections, HPV may not be totally eliminated from the body. Viral presence alone does not spread—lesions are required for transmission."[20] But if

Stacey comes across the book *What Your Doctor May* Not *Tell You About HPV and Abnormal PAP Smears*, she will find that the author, a leading expert, has a gloomier outlook: "Once you've been diagnosed with HPV . . . assume that you will always be infectious."[21]

When Stacey's Pap test returns to normal, will the virus be eliminated, or just dormant?[22] If she goes on the pill, could it increase the risk of cancer?[23] Why can pregnancy reactivate the virus?[24] We don't have definite answers to these questions.

What's next for Stacey? The gynecologist will do a culposcopy and biopsy, for which she'll lie with her feet in stirrups, and a large electric microscope will be positioned about a foot from her vagina. A bright light will illuminate her cervix, and the image of it will be projected on a screen. The doctor will decide what area looks abnormal, and then remove a bit of tissue. Then Stacey will wait two weeks to find out if the HPV she has is a cancer-causing one, and whether she needs another procedure or not.

Hopefully this isn't all taking place during finals. When you've got two papers to write and three exams to take, going in for a culposcopy and waiting for results is the last thing you want on your to-do list.

It's reasonable to assume that, for many college women, there's going to be some emotional fallout from this ordeal: the unexpected Pap results, the STD diagnosis, the mystery of when and from whom she got it, a second uncomfortable procedure, waiting for results, wondering about telling partners, ex-partners, and parents . . . all the while presumably going to classes, completing schoolwork, perhaps holding down a job, or commuting in traffic. Talk about stress!

Here's one gynecologist's experience: "The psychologic trauma is usually significant when the patient receives a diagnosis of HPV because she is often caught by surprise. Such a diagnosis was not suspected and the patient often feels taken advantage of, betrayed, or violated. . . . It is not uncommon for these patients to become angry and depressed."[25]

Others working with young women diagnosed with HPV try to help them "[overcome] feelings of shock and shame" so that they have "the psychological health necessary to cope with an abnormal Pap smear."[26] HPV may cause "significant emotional distress . . . anxiety about treatment, confusion and anger regarding sexual transmission, and feelings of guilt, blame, and fear." The virus "can have a powerful effect on one's self-concept and self-definition."

With so many college women finding out they carry this virus, campus health centers—like all women's health providers—are faced with a challenge. HPV infection is complex and brings many uncertainties. Will it be harmless or cause disease? Will it cause temporary distress, or major depression? Will her relationship survive or be destroyed? How does a health center provide thorough and accurate education, while avoiding mass hysteria? How do staff explain to a frightened and embarrassed young woman how she got this bug through her own decisions, without rubbing salt in her wounds?

Now the damage control begins. This is how pamphlets at student health centers deal with HPV: "HPV infection is very common . . . almost everyone gets HPV at some time. . . . having only a single lifetime partner does not assure protection. . . . *anyone* who has ever had sexual relations has a high chance of being exposed to this virus . . . most men and women are infected with HPV at some time in their lives."[27]

The calming message is: sure, you're upset—you could develop warts or cancer. But look at it this way: almost everyone's in the same boat. Unless you were thinking of lifelong abstinence, you were bound to get this bug at some point. So chill out, and welcome to the club.

These reassurances are inaccurate, and do no favor to women: in fact, infection with HPV is *completely preventable.* It is *not* an inevitable consequence of becoming sexually active. It is *not* something that will happen sooner or later. Even if well-intentioned, to imply otherwise is misleading.

This may not be popular to talk about, but there exists a population of young women and men who do not have to worry about HPV. Or, for that matter, about herpes, chlamydia, or HIV. They are safe because they wait, and marry someone else who waited. Yes, it can be done; people have been known to survive and tell others about it. Medicine should be studying *them,* and how they avoid risky behaviors, then applying that knowledge to our reproductive health education campaigns. Instead, there is an odd approach in sexual health: instead of asking our youth to strive for self-control and smart choices, we assume they'll make poor choices and have multiple partners, including some they hardly know. Why else would every pamphlet and Web site advise them, "First, talk with your partner." It's as if whoever's composing this material has given up on standards, and expects the behavior of the lowest common denominator. "Almost everyone gets HPV at some time,"[28] says a popular health Web site, implying: it's really not something to get upset about. Here's how one doctor, trying to provide words of comfort on an HPV support site, put it:

> *Your body is full of viruses. . . . Normal life not only involves colonization by microbes; it requires it. . . . Over 99% of our interactions with microbes are either neutral [or] they benefit us in some way; harm is rare. Also, there is nothing particularly special about the fact that a virus or other microbe is acquired sexually. Sex is simply one of the many ways in which humans interact with one another. All those interactions involve sharing bacteria, viruses, etc.*[29]

What? "One of the many ways in which humans interact with one another"? Is that the message we want to give to young people? Isn't that the precise philosophy that brought us this out-of-control epidemic? Forty years ago we had two sexually transmitted infections to worry about—now we have twenty-five. Is anyone else wondering what I am: What microscopic surprises are incubating today that we'll only discover tomorrow?

But some think all this worrying on my part is excessive—I'm an alarmist, causing unwarranted fear. And what about the good news about HPV—the vaccine now up for approval by the FDA? Yes, it is good news, it may even help Stacey, by boosting her immunity. Still, I don't think we should rely on medical technology for a quick fix to a social problem. Vaccine or not, my concerns are legitimate, and they are unwelcome, I believe, because they challenge campus dogma: latex protects, behaviors are entrenched, disease is unavoidable.

But these same health providers approach other risks differently: overeating, a sedentary lifestyle, smoking, drinking, driving without seat belts. With these topics, they emphatically endorse an ideal and aren't shy about sharing their expectations. They know their success will be limited, that some patients are in denial and won't listen, that others hear the warning but choose to live with the risk. Many make an effort, succeed for a while, then slip back to old habits. It's frustrating, to be sure, for health professionals, but they carry on, patiently and optimistically, working with patients to change their ways.

Why, then, when it comes to risky sexual behavior, do they settle for risk *reduction* instead of risk *elimination?* Why do they tiptoe around and worry about judging? They wouldn't settle for merely cutting down on tobacco; they hound students about stopping altogether, presenting their advice with sobering predictions and offering medication to curb cravings. Here's how one article recommended that physicians speak with adolescents and young adults who smoke:

> *Advise tobacco users to stop. . . . Mention reduced athletic capability, cost, stained fingers and teeth, cigarette burns and odors on clothes. . . . Congratulate every patient not using tobacco. . . . Discuss benefits of non-use. Share a few tobacco advertisements with the adolescent and point*

*out how they make the habit seem fun and sophisticated
but ignore all the unpleasant and harmful effects.*[30]

The approach to alcohol is similiarly aggressive and blunt.
Here's how to discourage binge drinking: "Present them
with as many facts as you can. Appeal to their vanity, tell
them drinking gives them bad breath and makes them
gain weight."[31]

The National Institute on Alcohol Abuse and Alco-
holism (NIAAA) created an eighty-six-page college drinking prevention curriculum, *Clinical Protocols to Reduce High
Risk Drinking in College Students,* to train campus health-
care providers to identify and treat students at risk. The
program is based on a "harm reduction public health para-
digm." It advises providers to have "treatment optimism"
and to "treat students on the premise that students will
change their drinking habits with clinical interventions,"
in spite of the fact that levels of use "have changed little over
the past twenty years on most campuses." A suggested opening question, to be asked "with empathy and interest," is
"Have you ever drunk or used drugs more than you meant
to?" Providers are reminded to "be sincere, be respectful,
establish trust, emphasize confidentiality."

So when it comes to tobacco and alcohol, concerted efforts to address "lifestyle" issues are an integral part of
medical care, and we make a point of sharing our values
and expectations with patients. Why not in sexual matters?
When we know that many students are, like Stacey, engaging in risky behavior, why not remind them of the sobering
facts, without sugarcoating them with "It's a very common

virus . . . most people get it at some point"? Where is the suggestion to "appeal to their vanity" and inform students that "STDs cause blisters and warts on your private parts that can't be cured"?

With 40 percent of college women experiencing a sexual encounter without commitment, and 10 percent reporting doing so more than six times,[32] where is the training for health and counseling staff to identify students at risk for unwanted pregnancy, STDs, and depression? Why no sincerely asked question during a routine visit such as, "Have you ever had a 'hookup'?" and why no empathic exploration of how awkward it feels the next morning?[33] Why no pamphlets in our waiting room directed at freshmen women, with data about their "increased vulnerability" in romance? Why the absence of material like this to motivate behavioral change, for women receiving results of a pregnancy test or STD screening:

> *You have been given an incredible gift.*
> *The test was* negative.
> *And now you have a chance to do something really*
>   positive.
> . . . You can do it. Start Now . . . *it's never too late to*
>   *start making*
> *Better decisions about your sexual health.*[34]

Why not explain to Heather, Olivia, and Stacey that they are more vulnerable to STDs than men are, and they will pay a higher price for getting one? True, Stacey is one of 5 million, but that doesn't mean it's less of a crisis; it means there are 5 million crises. The pamphlets and Web sites almost suggest that, if you're sexually active, the virus *belongs* in your system—how crazy is that? No, Stacey is correct to be shocked and upset. Even knowing the statistics, she'll always remember the moment she was told about having an STD. And because it *is* a big deal, a crisis, it's the perfect opportunity for a student-health practitioner to counsel her or at least provide self-help material about the medical reasons to change her lifestyle. Campus health services are in the ideal position to educate women about how their anatomy renders them vulnerable to infection.

Yes, their anatomy. Instead of the fringe behaviors endorsed—no, *promoted;* when you provide a directory of swing clubs or the Web site of an S&M group, you are promoting those behaviors—by Columbia University's "Alice," shouldn't the site instruct young women about an area of their cervix called "the transformation zone"? Surely the "health experts" running this site are aware that the cells here are more vulnerable to bacteria and viruses, and that with age, it shrinks.[35] How about providing photos and diagrams of the immature cervix in pamphlets and on Web sites, and on large posters hung on the walls of patient waiting areas? Why doesn't "Alice" explain to the young women at Columbia and elsewhere that being on the pill may enlarge the transformation zone, increasing the risk of infection? Perhaps this information might convince some campus women to delay sexual activity. Wouldn't that in fact be the *most* effective means of "limiting" their partners? If only 10 percent changed their behavior, that could mean hundreds of thousands spared an ordeal like Stacey's.

It makes you wonder what the priorities are in this field of medicine. Because if the priority is to guide women to avoid hazardous behavior, we can do better than this.

Here too, the doctrine of sex without consequences and the notion that women are just like men have made their way into the field of reproductive health, also called women's health. It's ironic—if the health of women were the sole concern here, they'd be screaming from the roof-tops of every planned parenthood and campus health center for women to wait, if only one or two years.

In their efforts to educate students, campus health and counseling centers lump men and women together. This is inaccurate in the extreme. Young women are more easily infected, and when "safer sex" fails, they pay big-time. The eighteen-year-old woman arriving on campus needs more than STD pamphlets, condoms, and prescriptions for birth control. Because she is more vulnerable, and pays a higher price if infected, there needs to be specialized outreach to her. This effort could draw from existing programs targeting college students, ones that address public health issues such as tobacco and alcohol use. *The message must get out: casual sex is a health hazard for young women.* Women must hear from campus authorities that delaying sex, even for one or two years, is a fundamental way—in addition to eating right, exercising, wearing sunscreen—to be proactive about their health. And why not offer support groups for students who want to change their behavior? Why not familiarize them with their anatomy, the research on bonding, and the risk of depression? Yes, this will highlight the differences between men and women, but shouldn't our daughters be warned?

Look at how different health decisions are valued. When Stacey avoids fatty foods, she is being health-conscious. When she turns down a cigarette, she is taking care of herself. When she stays aways from alcohol, she is being responsible and resisting her impulses. For all these, she is endorsed for keeping long-term goals in mind instead of giving in to peer pressure and immediate gratification. But if she makes a conscious decision to delay sexual acivity, she's simply "not sexually active"—given no praise or endorsement for her wise decision.

Sexual health information will typically have one-liners such as "abstaining from sexual contact is the surest way to avoid infection,"[36] or "for all STDs, abstinence is the best protection."[37] But they are like postscripts or disclaimers. Information is not presented as a viable alternative with considerable rewards; this would be moralizing and unrealistic. But forget right and wrong—with fifteen million new cases of STDs a year, delaying intercourse is sound *medical* advice. And if it's unrealistic to believe that our youth are smart and mature enough to make wise choices—not all of them all the time, but many of them much of the time—then the future is grim indeed.

I see it differently. The young people I know are neither stupid nor enslaved to their urges. They are capable and motivated; many will respond to an ennobling message, reject the prurient messages of our culture, and learn new behaviors. Isn't that what youth is about—questioning, idealism, change? But for this to happen, we must tell the whole story, warts and all. Tell them we're waging a war against these bugs, and the bugs are winning. Tell them 20 million people in our country have HPV, mostly women and minorities, and that doctors, drug companies, and corporations are making billions.[38] Tell them this contributes to skyrocketing health insurance. Tell them their behavior, and their friends', can make a difference. Tell them the truth!

A delusion is "a false belief that is resistant to reason or confrontation with actual fact."[39] I submit that "safer sex" is a delusion, one that especially imperils young women on campus. We need to come clean, and fully disclose to our youth the dreadful consequences of behaviors encouraged by our culture, so they can make fully informed decisions. The only people who are completely safe are those who, along with their spouses, waited for marriage, and once married, remain faithful. The ones who are "safer" delay sexual behavior, discriminate carefully in their choice, and understand the weight of their decisions. We don't hesitate, in other areas of health, to strive toward an ideal. Why, with Stacey and millions of others, do we settle for so much less?

CHAPTER III

MEMO TO THE APA:
BELIEVING IN GOD IS GOOD FOR YOU

WHAT'S THE MATTER WITH NED? HE CAN'T SAY WHAT'S BOTHERING him. An MBA student, blond and clean-cut, he tries to explain why he's come, but I'm still waiting.

What could it be? Students confide in me about all sorts of misbehavior and foul play, and they do it without hesitation. I've heard about cheating, plagiarism, shoplifting, forgeries, infidelities, and property destruction. Students report on their DUIs, arrests, dismissal from school. They all manage to spit it out. So what's Ned's problem?

"I don't think you'll understand," he says. "I'm Catholic. I'm married, and I love my wife."

I wait.

"We're happy together, and we want to start a family soon."

I wait again.

"There's something I do that I want to stop. . . . It may not sound like much to you, but for me it's awful—and it causes my wife pain."

He looks at me.

"I have urges to look at pictures of women. Sometimes I give in and go online, or I buy a magazine. Not pornography—maybe the *Sports Illustrated* bathing suit edition or a Victoria's Secret catalog. I've confessed, I've prayed, I've even fasted, and nothing has helped. You probably don't think it's a big deal. But I want to stop—it's not Christian, and it hurts my wife . . . can you understand?"

This is his lucky day, I thought.

"Yes, I understand. I'm religious too. My son would feel the same way."

His mouth drops, and his eyes open wide. "You *are?* He *would?* Wow—that's *great!*"

Ned had expected a culture clash. He'd assumed I'd think him overscrupulous, his religiosity extreme. Although wrong in this particular instance, Ned's instincts were correct: most psychiatrists and psychologists do not share his worldview.[1] Ned's whole approach to life—like that of three-quarters of Americans—is based on his faith. His relationship with Jesus is central, and he turns to the church for guidance. But a majority of clinical psychologists have left the religion of their upbringing, and they rarely attend religious services.[2] In one survey, a majority characterized their beliefs and practices as an "alternative spiritual path which is not a part of an organized religion."[3] In another, 25 percent of psychologists thought God is "a product of human imagination."[4]

How do these numbers compare with the religious identification of other highly educated professionals? In one survey,[5] university faculty were asked about their current religion, and the percentage in each department saying "none" was compared. Fifty percent of psychology faculty had no religion, as compared to 27 percent of physicians and 16 percent of dentists. Compared to the general population, psychologists are almost five times more likely to be agnostic or atheist.[6] When a therapist thinks her client follows an extreme ideology—especially when it is an ideology opposite to hers—it can affect her personal response and clinical judgment in a negative way.[7] She may consider the client more disturbed and less mature; she might not like him as much, and the therapy could be less successful.

Ned was relieved to have me as his doctor. I learned of other compulsive behaviors, and suggested medication. We spoke about the importance of prayer and hope, and agreed that while we both need to do everything we can, ultimately a cure comes from above.

While Ned was surprised to find a religious psychiatrist, I found him unusual as well. Having worked with university students for years, I take in stride the pierced lips and tongues, the tattoos, shaved heads, or dreadlocks. I'm not surprised when students can only estimate the number of sexual partners they've had or admit to using hallucinogens, passing out from alcoholic binges, or picking up strangers in bars. I am (fairly) comfortable with a patient who appears to be male, but has breasts and menstruates.

Ned, in contrast, values chastity and self-restraint. He prays, gives to charity, and strives for godliness in his life. After abstaining from sex, he married his high school sweetheart and now wants to be a father. Now *that's* strange.

Reading the campus newspaper—or the pamphlets in our waiting room—suggests that for most students, affairs of the spirit are the last thing on their minds. It would appear that students are primarily concerned about their sexual health and identity, drugs and alcohol, academic success, learning how to relax, and getting enough sleep. Not that those issues aren't important, but the results of a national study of thousands of college students support a different conclusion.[8] Over three-quarters of students said they pray, and nearly as many report they are "searching for meaning and purpose in life."

Prayer, meaning, purpose—on our college campuses? Who would've guessed? And here I thought young people just wanted to get good grades and avoid genital warts!

The study also indicates that students who are highly involved in religion report better mental health: non-church-going students are seven times more likely to feel overwhelmed, nearly three times more likely to rate themselves "below average" in emotional health, and twice as likely to report depression or psychological distress. How do the researchers define "religious involvement"? These are the students who read sacred texts, attend religious services, and join religious organizations on campus.[9]

Sarah is one such student. She studies the Book of Mormon daily and is immersed in church activities. She told me the following story.

Sarah called the student health center for an appointment. She and her husband wanted another child, but Sarah needed medication in order to conceive. "This is the right time for us to try," she explained. "If I don't take the medication soon, it may be many months until our next opportunity. Could someone please see me in the next day or two?" No, she was told, the next available appointment for that is in two months. "Two months!—but all I need is a prescription, I've used it before, and it's on my record. Are you sure?" Yes, I'm sorry, two months.

She hung up, upset and frustrated. Then she had an idea, and called again. "Hello, I need an appointment to get some birth control." It was eleven o'clock. Birth control? Sure, when do you want to come? I have 11:30, 12, 12:30 . . .

She took the twelve o'clock. After all, Sarah told me, it *was* birth control—but of a different sort: she *wanted* a baby!

You have five children, why would you want to get pregnant? the physician asked. "Because I want another child!" Sarah explained. The doctor didn't buy it. "You don't need help ovulating," she announced, "you need birth control." And she left the room.

Stunned and hurt, Sarah sang a hymn to herself, and was able to calm down. She reminded herself that the decision to have a child is between a husband, a wife, and the Lord. She didn't need anyone else's approval. She focused on the teaching that bearing a child is a great blessing, the noblest calling for a woman. When the doctor returned, Sarah tried a different approach. "I hope to go to law school next year," she said, "and I want to have one more child before I start." The doctor weighed this new information. Law school? You're going to law school? "Yes," Sarah told her. She got the medicine.

"What a shocking story," I said to her. "What an ordeal. How did you feel?"

"I'm used to it. I expect those people to give me a hard time. It's like asking an abused woman how she felt the tenth time she's beaten."

Let's compare Sarah's experience with the tolerance on campus of another student. Kris, a chemistry major, came to see me for evaluation. He is on his way to becoming a man: his beard is coming in, and his voice is changing. But it's not what you think—Kris is not a boy becoming a man. Kris—aka Kristina—is a *woman* becoming a man.

Kris's appearance is rather odd at the moment: he has the start of a beard and mustache as well as large breasts. I am touched by the story of his journey, and impressed with his intelligence, humor, and courage. Some people might feel awkward and unsure of how to relate to him, but I'm at ease—I attended a program at the university about transgenders. A workshop was held for the counseling center staff, to sensitize us to the unique issues facing this group. There was a guest speaker, a therapist with expertise in counseling "trans folk," and a female-to-male transgender described his experience and took questions. I heard about childhood struggles, hormone treatments, surgical procedures, hate crimes, and discrimination. I learned about "Patriot Act Hell"—documents like driver's licenses and school records cannot be changed. One's birth name and sex are still there, so one is automatically "outed." I was informed of the proper language to use: to say "chest surgery," not "mastectomies." When I'm not clear whether a patient wants to be considered male or female, I was taught, I should ask.

I learned that the "gender binary system" of male/female isn't accurate; that the male whose sense of himself is that he is a man, is masculine, and is attracted only to women, and the woman whose sense of self is that she is female, is feminine, and is attracted only to men, are "stereotypes." My colleagues and I were gently advised to "start with ourselves, and examine how we are programmed into a binary gender system," and to reject it, because "we all benefit from breaking down the gender binary."

I'm glad I attended the program. My "cultural competency" got a boost—even if I don't agree with the ideology. I am now better equipped to care for Kris and the other .08 percent of students on campus to whom these issues are relevant.

"Cultural competency" is very big right now in health promotion, especially campus health. The American College Health Association's *Cultural Competency Statement* declares,

> *We . . . believe that healthy communities must be guided by the values of inclusion, respect, and equality. Intolerance and subtler forms of insensitivity or exclusion have no place at an institution of higher learning. . . . We therefore commit to: Foster an inclusive, affirming, and respectful climate. . . . Promote the cultural competence of individuals and organizations with respect to race/ ethnicity, gender, sexual orientation, disability, religion, and other identities. . . . Engage in the personal and professional growth required to embrace individual and institutional diversity. . . . Through these efforts we will enhance our services, foster our own personal and professional development, and advance the health of all students.*[10]

Now, if "cultural competency" is a valid concept in health and psychology (and some question that[11]), it's fair to ask: where do Ned and Sarah fit in? Given the tsunami of calls for tolerance, diversity, and multiculturalism, given the policy statements, declarations, ethically mandated culturally sensitive behavior, training programs, professional requirements, and hiring preferences, it's fair to wonder: when is the workshop sensitizing staff to beliefs and practices of strict Roman Catholics, Mormons, Evangelicals, Baptists, and Orthodox Jews?[12] When will health and counseling center staff be told to examine their own misconceptions and bias, and to recognize the offensive and sometimes hostile experiences a religious student faces on campus?

Ned wants to know: Is there a therapist here who shares his values and lifestyle? He believes abortion and homosexuality are forbidden—do we have a psychologist or social worker who won't automatically label him a religious extremist and a homophobe? Sarah asks: Is there a counselor whose own life is pious and disciplined, who can identify with her and the lifestyle she's embraced—patriarchal family and all? And I wonder: What efforts are being made, pursuant to the calls for inclusion and affirmation, to increase the sensitivity and respect for *these* students and their culture—a culture that believes God created the world, and gave us rules to live by?

I once asked about this, when our center had an open position for a social worker. I suggested to a collegue, who I knew to be a dedicated, compassionate psychiatrist, that perhaps we could recruit a therapist from a community of faith. Students making appointments sometimes ask for a Christian therapist, and in fact, I said, thinking of Ned, I am seeing a student right now who prefers a counselor who shares his religious values. Well, he answered, any of our therapists could work with him, because a good therapist is able to work with clients whose values differ from theirs. He added that he, a biracial man, once counseled a client who was sympathetic to the Klan, and it was difficult, but he was able to do it. That may be so, I said. Still, in the past we've recruited applicants who were gay or lesbian, or belonged to racial minorities because our staff is supposed to reflect the diversity of the campus. And there is a subpopulation of students on our campus who are from fundamentalist religious communities.[13] So isn't it reasonable to recruit a therapist with expertise in working with those clients? "No," he said, "I don't believe we are allowed to do that."

Let's look at this closely. Ned and Sarah have paid their registration fees and student insurance premiums, just like other students. These monies fund our center. Like everyone else, they are entitled to nonjudgmental, culture-affirming health care. But unlike a Latino, black, or lesbian student, students like Ned and Sarah will not find a therapist at the student counseling center with their conservative social values. And unlike Kris, Sarah—now joyfully pregnant with her sixth child—avoids the health center, because of her painful and offensive encounters there. You see, the doctors, nurses, and ancillary staff there are aware of the medical needs of the transgendered student, and they won't be thrown off when a male student comes in for his yearly Pap smear. But are they sensitized to the needs of devout women like Sarah? Are they encouraged to embrace and respect her minority, in which the job of "family planning" is given over to God, and every child is welcomed as a gift and a blessing? Yes, even a sixth pregnancy. Because in Sarah's culture, in *her* community, there are no "unwanted pregnancies." The very concept is offensive and distressing.

"If it wasn't for Jesus, I wouldn't be here anymore. I'm sure of it." That's how Melodie answered when I asked what kept her going. She's a twenty-year-old Asian American woman, an accomplished tennis player who can't play due to a series of injuries. She also has financial and academic stressors. But when Melodie felt like jumping off a building, her beliefs stood in the way.

Like many people with strong religious faith, Melodie is less likely to end her life.[14] Believing the body sacred, and suicide a sin, restrains her from self-destructive behavior. But it's not only fear of punishment that has saved Melodie. It's also hope, and meaning.

When it comes to preventing suicide, hope is a very big deal. All things being equal—the depth of a depression, the severity of life events—the presence or lack of hope can mean the difference between life and death.[15] Melodie draws hope from the Gospel of Luke and Psalms. She carries a Bible in her backpack. Sometimes she prays between classes. Paxil and cognitive therapy notwithstanding, Melodie credits her survival to her church: it has had the most profound influence on her struggle. I agree.

Sincere devotion and frequent participation in a religious community benefits mental health.[16] A place of worship provides structure, a community, and meaningful relationships. Religious commitment encourages healthy behaviors, such as avoidance of smoking, alcohol, drug use, and sex outside of marriage. By lowering disease risk, it increases well-being. Prayer and other rituals are associated with positive emotions like empowerment, contentment, self-esteem, and love. Most important, regardless of faith and denomination, sincere religious devotion infuses life with depth, meaning, and hope—the polar opposites of the emptiness and despair associated with suicide. Indeed, the intolerable mental pain of meaninglessness has been called "the essence of the suicidal mind."[17]

Large numbers of studies, performed at secular medical schools and schools of public health, indicate that practicing a mainstream faith confers significant health benefits. People who use "religious coping"—prayer, confession, seeking strength and comfort from God—adjust better to stressful life events such as kidney transplant, cancer, the Oklahoma City bombing, the death of a close friend, and the loss of a child through sudden infant death.[18] Devotion and participation in a religious community significantly decrease the likelihood of depression in at-risk adolescent girls.[19] In a survey of nearly 35,000 adolescents, religiousness was inversely associated with dangerous behaviors: binge drinking, marijuana use, cigarette smoking, and premarital sex.[20] A study of children whose parents had severe mental illness showed some were strengthened by "the sense of incorporating something larger than oneself." To the researchers' astonishment, some of these children climbed to success and health through intense affiliations with religious groups.[21] Frequency of prayer is associated with long survival in persons with HIV/AIDS.[22] Religiosity and spirituality is associated with lower blood pressure in older adults.[23] Attending religious services once a week may be a more cost-effective way of living longer than taking cholesterol-lowering medication.[24] After studying the relationship between attending religious services and mortality, a professor of preventive medicine concluded: "I think I'll go to church."[25] Yes, people who go to church live longer.[26]

Attitudes fostered by religious or spiritual paths have been examined, and Ph.D.s confirm what common sense already tells us: forgiveness promotes personal and marital happiness; gratitude contributes to well-being; and optimism is associated with better outcomes.[27]

Now don't get me wrong. I've written plenty of prescriptions for devout patients who struggle with debilitating sadness, obsessions, violent outbursts, or psychotic episodes. Members of religious communities, like everyone else, suffer from every symptom in the book—I refer here to psychiatry's bible, *Diagnostic and Statistical Manual of Mental Disorders*, or DSM-IV. Some ministers beat their wives, some rabbis abuse children, some Catholics commit suicide. But these facts do not justify the omission by therapists of faith as a potential source of meaning and comfort for their distressed clients.

One NIH researcher wrote, "Results . . . have been consistent in indicating a salutary relationship between religious involvement and health status. . . . This finding has been observed in studies of old, middle-aged, and young respondents; in men and women; in subjects from the United States, Europe, Africa; in research conducted in the 1930's and into the 1990's; in case-control, prospective cohort, cross-sectional, and panel studies; in Protestants, Catholics, Jews, Muslims, Buddhists, Parsis, and Zulus."[28]

Memo to the American Psychological and Psychiatric

associations: Believing in God is good for you. A sense of meaning and purpose benefits mental health. It toughens the skin, and softens the blows of life. To know there is a larger plan, to believe that events are not random, and that you and your behavior *matter*—this can soothe and heal. To have gratitude and hope, to forgive oneself and others, and to connect with something greater than oneself though prayer and ritual—this is great medicine, maybe even better than Zoloft. And mind you—I *love* Zoloft; I've prescribed tons of it.

Given the very strong evidence that religious faith is associated with health benefits, especially mental health, one would expect doctors, nurses, and therapists to be reminding their patients about it 24/7. But think back: has your internist ever mentioned that optimists have stronger immune systems, or that churchgoers live longer? Has your family therapist told you that religion protects against adolescent drug and alcohol use, early sexual activity, and suicide?

Probably not. Medical providers typically ignore the role of faith in health maintenance. Psychotherapists do too. It's fair to say, in fact, that in mainstream clinical psychology, religion is taboo.

A book could be written on this alone, but a few examples will have to do. Consider that psychology is the study of the mind—thought, emotion, and behavior. Polls consistently show that about 95 percent of Americans believe in God, almost 90 percent pray to God at least occasionally, and about 60 percent attend a place of worship monthly.[29] Eighty-five percent consider religion "very important or fairly important" in their lives, and 80 percent believe religion strengthens family life.[30] Religious beliefs predict behavior more than race, education, or economic status. Religious beliefs are protective against suicide,[31] substance abuse, and risky sexual behavior. Now consider:

- A search in the indexes of several recently published, authoritative psychology and psychiatry textbooks, four of them focused on suicide, reveals no entries for church, religion, prayer, or God.[32]
- When psychology textbooks discuss religion, it is often with a focus on religious pathology, like the Jonestown mass suicide, Waco, or pedophilia in the Catholic Church.[33]
- A past president of the American Psychological Association called on psychologists to help get rid of organized religion. "It doesn't matter which religion, they are all patriarchal. And that is one of the major sources of social injustice in our society and in our world."[34]
- In a list of forty-eight questions that the APA advises psychiatrists to use in assessing suicidal patients, none concerns ultimate issues such as purpose, meaning, the soul, or an afterlife.[35]
- A review of seven major journals of the American Psychological Association showed an average of only 2.7 percent of studies considered religion as a research variable.[36] A search of two broad social science databases, Social Science Abstracts and PsycINFO, for articles addressing spirituality among children

and adolescents, showed this topic was given attention in less than 1 percent of studies.[37] There is an astonishing neglect of religion in academic research.
The R word may in fact be an "anti-tenure factor."[38]
- Conservatives are vastly underrepresented in psychology, and their views marginalized. One study
showed that identifying as a fundamentalist Christian made it harder to get into a graduate program
in psychology.[39] A psychologist and lawyer working in
public policy laments the lack of sociopolitical diversity in psychology, and suggests reaching out through
affirmative-action-like practices to conservatives in
graduate student recruiting and faculty hiring.[40]

There is a name for the irrational antagonism that psychology has for religion: *theophobia*. I suggest that most
psychologists,[41] who themselves have made a conscious decision to leave the faith of their upbringing and whose
circle of professional and personal associates consists mostly
of secular, humanistic persons like themselves, experience
discomfort discussing God and other ultimate issues, and
therefore avoid them. Such topics, they mistakenly believe,
are important only to a small fringe group. These highly
trained professionals hold stereotyped views of religious
people as uneducated and primitive. Why would a self-
realized, fully mature person turn to the pope for guidance? How can an intelligent adult believe that the world
was created in six days? Why would a woman living in
this century have ten children? The notion that God hears
and responds to prayers is childish. Fundamentalists must

be disturbed. These prejudices and misconceptions are rooted in psychologists' own ignorance, guilt, fears, and insecurities.

Theophobia is endemic to campus health and counseling; issues of faith are absent in the evaluation and treatment of distressed college students.[42] For example, the initial interview with a student includes many questions, some of them deeply personal: *Do you drink too much? Have you ever been suicidal or homicidal? What method of birth control do you use? Are you questioning your sexual orientation? Was there verbal, physical, or sexual abuse in your family?* And some of them not: *Do you smoke? How much coffee, tea, and soda do you drink?* But these are absent: *What gives your life meaning? Do you believe in God? For what do you pray?*

These questions are vital. They are just as important as the routine questions about alcohol, drugs, cigarettes, caffeine, sleep, exercise, and abuse. When first meeting a patient, therapists are urged not to assume heterosexuality. This would be evidence of "heterosexism," says the APA. It's essential for a therapist to *ask* about sexual orientation; the patient may not offer the information on his own. But the neglect of a patient's religious beliefs also makes an assumption: the patient has none. By omitting faith and existential issues from her work, a therapist deems them irrelevant, putting her dangerously out of sync with some students, and losing a potentially powerful component of treatment. With Prozac the number-one prescribed medication on college campuses,[43] and with about 1,100 student suicides each year, this is alarming indeed.

Acknowledgment of the role of religion in students'

lives is also strangely absent from a recent book, *College of the Overwhelmed*.[44] The authors, one of whom is chief of the Mental Health Service at Harvard University Health Services and a national expert in the field of campus mental health, write in their introduction, "This is a book about the extraordinary increase in serious mental illness on college campuses today and what we can do about it." College students are stressed to their limits, they explain. They face many challenges: leaving home, competing for grades, getting along with roommates, dealing with relationships, sexuality. There are parental pressures and cultural expectations. The job market is shrinking, and there is a post-9/11 culture of fear. For some students, it's simply more than they can handle. Therefore the dramatic increase in depression, eating disorders, self-mutilation, substance abuse, and suicide. What to do? In the sixty-page section of the book titled "The Solution," the authors advise: Universities must strengthen student counseling services. Parents must improve communication, know warning signals, and be proactive. Students have to take better care of themselves (exercise, drink enough water, choose healthy snacks, sleep well . . .), stay connected with family, learn to manage their time, and know when to ask for help.

The authors seem oblivious to affairs of the spirit, at least in this book. Do they not recognize this deeper dimension of their patients, the drive to find meaning and purpose and to connect with something greater than themselves? Is it not relevant to their topic that spirituality in college students tempers the impact of stressful events?[45] That young adults returning from two years of missionary work had higher self-esteem, and greater purpose in life?[46]

What about the evidence supporting the protective quality of personal devotion in the mental health of adolescents? And what about the essential role of hope, meaning, and purpose in deterring post-traumatic stress disorder[47] and suicide? Is not part of the solution for the "College of the Overwhelmed" to include faith as a possible *resource,* an *ally* for counselors?

Likewise, pamphlets and Web sites of campus health and counseling centers omit the health benefits of mainstream religious beliefs and worship. Students are fed the usual mantras about health promotion through diet, exercise, sleep, calcium, breast exams, condoms, smoking cessation, seat belts ... The counseling centers emphasize healthy relationships, self-assertion, time management, making time for fun. These are all valid, but well-being goes beyond cholesterol levels and hours of sleep. Many young people ache to have ultimate issues asked and answered. Many actually believe they have a soul, and that to reach well-being on the deepest level, it too demands proper nourishment and protection.

As much as mental health professionals and organizations may shun issues of faith due to theophobia, 75 percent[48] of college students are on a spiritual search and seek answers to existential questions. Sounds like a large population, but it shouldn't come as a surprise; it's consistent with research indicating that neurologically, we may be designed to search for meaning.

You probably haven't heard about it. Two neuroscientists at the University of Pennsylvania used radioactive imaging to study the brain's capacity for spiritual experience.[49] They scanned the heads of skilled Tibetan meditators and Franciscan nuns following a period of intense religious contemplation, and discovered an unusual pattern of brain activity. As peak moments approached, the circuits responsible for orientation in time and space fell quiet. The area of the brain that informs us where we end, and the rest of the world starts, was turned off. These moments, according to the subjects, were accompanied by a rush of positive emotion. They were moments of "being connected to all of creation," of "a sense of timelessness and infinity" and "a tangible sense of the closeness of God and a mingling with Him." The researchers suggest that the brain is equipped from birth with a capacity—even an urge—for religious experience, and they call the study of this capacity "neurotheology." They even admit,

> *our research has left us no choice but to conclude that the mystics may be on to something, that the mind's machinery of transcendence may in fact be a window through which we can glimpse the ultimate realness of something that is truly divine. This conclusion is based on deductive reason, not on religious faith—it is a terrifically unscientific idea that is ironically consistent with careful, conventional science.*

It seems to me that psychology had better get its act together. The irrational avoidance of religion in therapeutic work is not only unethical, it's old. It has no place in this century, where single-photon emission computed tomography identifies "neuronal spirituality circuits" and produces color photos of a brain connecting with God.

I am not suggesting that psychotherapists get training

in pastoral counseling. Rather, they might at least *inquire* about a client's beliefs and, if appropriate, *inform* the client about the health-promoting effects of regular practice and *facilitate* his growth in this area. Otherwise, a powerful inner resource is untapped, and the therapeutic work is handicapped. For those who are searching, there are books such as *Man's Search for Meaning* (2 million sold), *The Road Less Traveled* (7 million sold), and *The Purpose-Driven Life* (20 million sold).[50] Yes, some students need to be reminded to take care of themselves. But many would benefit from being *less* self-absorbed, not *more*. Along with a prescription for medication, counselors should more often consider a referral to a priest or rabbi with expertise in working with young adults. One does not replace the other. They need to both be on the radar screen. When mental health professionals overlook such an integral dimension of people, they make a dangerous blunder.

But we don't know if God even exists, some may argue. To that I answer: no matter. Call it what you like, "a higher consciousness," "universal wisdom," "the transcendent," whatever. The point is, the yearning to know it exists, our neural machinery can mediate it, and the experience is a positive one. We don't know all the details yet, but these moments of a different reality can be health-promoting, and should be encouraged in a willing patient. We don't really know how aspirin works either, but we still consider it a wonder drug.

When survivors of catastrophic events, like war or the death of a child, are asked how they survived, some credit their faith in God. In the midst of calamity and suffering, they say, life still had meaning. Even in the worst of circumstances there were moments of hope. This kept them going. If belief in life's meaning and purpose helped concentration camp prisoners endure, it seems reasonable to assume these may be of some utility to college students unable to cope with finals and roommates. With a vast majority of college freshmen believing in God, it's time campus psychologists move beyond their own issues, and make room for Him in their work.

CHAPTER IV

SAVING PATIENT BRIAN

BRIAN HAS TWO PROBLEMS. FOR THE FIRST HE WANTS HELP; for the second he doesn't. Brian complains that he is addicted to cigarettes. It's bad for his health, expensive, and stinks up the car. His boyfriend hates it. So Brian has decided to quit—this time for real—using medication. That's why he made an appointment with me.

In the course of our discussion I learn that Brian, an English major, and his partner, an actor, often pick up other men. "It's hard to be monogamous," he explains. Neither uses protection, and Brian has never been tested for HIV. He does not discuss HIV status with his casual partners, or with his boyfriend. The topic of safer sex makes him nervous, and he'd rather not think about it.

I hear many fascinating tales at the counseling center. Students share the intimate details of their lives and struggles, and it's not boring. Nevertheless, once I'm behind the wheel of my car at the end of the day, my thoughts are no longer with my patients. Rarely do I bring my work home.

Brian is an exception. I can't get him off my mind. Brian, his boyfriend, and their partners may all be, or soon may be, infected with a lethal virus.

Remembering our meeting, I realize that my face betrayed my alarm, because Brian was quick to acknowledge his irresponsibility. Notably, he also said I was the first physician to discuss this topic with him—an astonishing fact, given Brian's openness about his orientation. I want to tell him he is endangering his life and that he must change his behavior at once. He must be tested and, if necessary, begin treatment. But I proceed gingerly, fearing that I might spook him and lose him as a patient. I remind myself that he did not present for help with this dangerous behavior, but rather for his tobacco addiction. So Brian and I discuss problem number one, but I also encourage him to limit his contacts and to use protection. We agree to meet again. Brian thanks me cordially and leaves. I remain alarmed: when we meet again, will he be newly infected?

There must be something else I can do to protect my patient. But what? I consult with a social worker on the staff who specializes in gay and lesbian issues. Maybe Stan has heard these stories too many times, because he sighs with resignation and suggests I refer Brian to a gay and lesbian health center off campus. But I don't want to refer Brian. He is my patient, my responsibility, and I want to see this through. A colleague at the student wellness center is sympathetic, but can offer no solution. "It's an uncomfortable ethical dilemma for physicians," he says. "You can only recommend testing and discourage unsafe activities. Your hands are tied unless you know someone is positive."

My hands are tied? Since when? I am often called upon to protect my patients, or those they could harm, and the law is on my side. If a patient is suicidal, homicidal, or gravely disabled I can involuntarily commit him. When a patient threatens to harm someone, the law obligates me to inform the police, and to warn the potential victim. When I see a suspicious bruise or burn on a minor, or discover that a child is not getting routine health or dental care or adequate adult supervision, state law requires that I report suspected abuse or neglect. In fact, I can suffer civil—and sometimes criminal—penalties for failing to do so.

My job is to treat and prevent disease, injury, and suffering. Rarely, my efforts may even play some part in saving a life. I am not accustomed to being told my hands are tied.

I visit the men's health department at the student wellness center. In the waiting area, I find an assortment of fact sheets, including two about HIV/AIDS. Here I learn that "1 in every 500 US college students, and 1 in every 330 of our students may be HIV positive." Let's see—with our student population, that's scores of infected people on campus. Posing the question, "Should I take an antibody test?" the flyer declares: "This is an individual and very personal decision. A number of factors should be considered, including risk for infection as well as one's ability to emotionally handle a potential positive result." How many students, aside from Brian, will find in these words justification for avoiding the blood test, depriving themselves of life-prolonging treatment and contributing to the virus's rampage?

On my way out of the student wellness center, I pick up a copy of the newsmagazine of the Lesbian Gay Bisexual Transgender group on campus. How do they address this critical issue? Turning the pages, I make another disturbing discovery. While I wring my hands over Brian's risky behavior, this publication provides coverage of a recent

"Leather Weekend," which featured among other events a "live bondage demonstration" and a "Fetish Vendor Mart." In the travel section, a review of Manhattan bars offers this tip:

> *The queen of the local gay house scene, Roxy . . . , is a cool dance club. . . . Beware the "Balcony" at the far end of the club; it stays dark for a reason. You can be sitting up there and chilling, and the next thing you know, someone is unbuttoning your pants.*

I want to scream. *But there's an epidemic raging—haven't you heard? There are 60,000 men in New York City with HIV or AIDS!*[1] *Thank you for letting my patient know where they hang out.*

I look up our HIV/AIDS laws in a guide provided by our state department of health. "The Office of AIDS is committed to assess, prevent, and interrupt the transmission of HIV," the first paragraph reads. Sounds good. Yet what follows is more about protecting the infected than the healthy: prohibitions against mandatory testing, insurance discrimination, and disclosure of HIV status in worker's compensation cases. HIV-infected persons, considered disabled, are also protected by federal and state statutes that prohibit discrimination in employment, housing, and public accommodations. The Health and Safety Code requires the reporting of a positive HIV test to the local health officer, using a "non-name code" to assure anonymity to the infected person.[2] The code permits, but does not require, notification of exposed contacts. The notification process, however, must not identify the HIV-infected person. So if one of Brian's partners was HIV positive, my patient would be in a position to be informed of his exposure only if the infected person appeared for voluntary testing and if he or his physician decided to notify others.

I am not reassured.

On the Centers for Disease Control's Web site (Division of HIV/AIDS Prevention) I find information about health education and risk reduction.[3] The document emphasizes the need for nonjudgmental patient care and reminds me that "disenfranchised minorities" are suspicious and distrustful of public health officials. In particular, "for African Americans, the Tuskegee Study continues to cast its own specter of doubt as to whether or not public health officials are truly committed to ensuring the public's health." Basically, they argue that "respect and regard for the perceptions of those being served will help eliminate barriers to HIV protection and will build the bridges to better health." The behavior known to be the easiest and most common sexual route of HIV transmission, anal intercourse, is not even mentioned.

I come across an editorial in a psychiatric newsmagazine: "The Challange of HIV Testing." The author, director of the division of HIV/AIDS prevention at the CDC, reports that in the United States there are 40,000 new infections a year, and about 900,000 people living with the disease. One quarter of these are unaware of their infection. I learn that only 10 percent of men get tested on the recommendation of a health-care provider, and that of those who are tested, many do not return to get their results. In response to this "clearly unacceptable" trend, the author suggests that providers "take time to talk regularly with patients about HIV testing and possible risk factors," offer the test more often to certain patients, and use the recently introduced rapid tests that give results on the spot.[4]

OK, but I'm afraid this won't help me save Brian.

My next stop is at the Gay and Lesbian Medical Association.[5] Surely they are concerned about protecting their own. One of the reasons for the continuing increases in HIV incidence, I am informed, is the poor interpersonal skills of health providers. Both patients and physicians feel awkward discussing the topic. Prevention messages do not get through. On a positive note, guidelines are offered for conducting sensitive and nonjudgmental assessments by providers.

Lastly, the county department of health offers me a 113-page document: *HIV Prevention Program*. It appears they are following in the CDC's footsteps, taking prevention one step further. Here, I learn that fighting oppression can prevent HIV. Racism, homophobia, AIDS discrimination, and stigma—these are the culprits permitting the deadly virus to propagate.

Racism? Oppression? Where did this come from? In medical school, I learned that there are standard procedures for fighting epidemics. Using traditional public health control tools, we, in the developed world at least, have somehow managed to bring under control horrific diseases such as cholera, polio, and syphilis. This apparently was achieved without pouring billions of taxpayer dollars into programs promoting cultural sensitivity. Yet this was in the pre-AIDS era: I took the Hippocratic oath a year before the identification of gay-related immune deficiency syndrome, as it was originally designated in 1981.

And speaking of the Hippocratic oath, I swore "to prevent disease whenever I can," and to "remember that I remain a member of society, with special obligations to all my fellow human beings." These responsibilities I take to heart. And that's why, as I drive home today, I am racked by a sense of helplessness. What can I do to prevent my patient from acquiring and transmitting an infection that will likely kill him in the prime of his life? Why does the university allow students to publish material that promotes high-risk behavior, while adopting a touchy-feely approach to testing—calling it "a personal decision," to be done only "if you can emotionally handle it"? Do they have the same concerns for a student who finds a lump somewhere—"Do the biopsy only if you have fortitude, it's a personal decision"? Why is legislation focused on protecting the rights of the infected at the expense of the uninfected?

HIV infection is entirely preventable. It seems reasonable to advocate that those who are HIV-positive must be promptly identified and treated, and that the healthy must be protected. Fighting stigma and oppression is important, but if existing measures for combating this epidemic are not implemented, Brian—like the 500,000 AIDS victims before him—is doomed. Does anyone care?

Tom arrived on campus six months ago from South Korea, to get his Ph.D. in electrical engineering. Like many international students, he comes from a country where tuberculosis is endemic. Tom looks and feels fine, but he could still be carrying the bacteria, and at any point he could suddenly get sick. If that happens, it could be bad news for his roommates.

Tuberculosis and HIV have some things in common. Let's say Brian has HIV, and Tom has TB. They may both be infected, capable of infecting others, and not know it. Both benefit from early detection, since they're most responsive to treatment at that time. Others benefit too, as this is a time of high infectivity. Without treatment, they may become seriously—fatally—ill.

There are also profound differences between the two infections: their mode of transmission, incidence, and prognosis. TB is airborne, HIV is transmitted sexually, by sharing needles, or during birth and nursing. The records for my state show that in 2002, there were more than eight cases of HIV for every case of TB. Tuberculosis is almost always cured, but HIV becomes AIDS, which is fatal.

Another difference between HIV and TB is how I, as a health-care provider, am expected to manage patients at risk.

Brian has told me about his dangerous behavior. As we speak, he may be highly infectious, with a virus level that's through the roof. My role is to urge him to be tested, to openly and honestly discuss his HIV status with his boyfriend, to limit his casual contacts, and to use condoms.

It's another story with TB. If Tom recently lived with an infected relative and was never screened, I am expected to give him a tuberculin skin test. If it's positive, he gets a chest X-ray. This is standard medical care. If the skin test and X-ray lead me to suspect that Tom may have tuberculosis, I am obligated by law to report him to the Department of Health, and I have one working day to do so. I must fill out a confidential morbidity report giving his name, date of birth, social security number, address, phone number, occupation, country of birth, date he arrived in the United States, race, and ethnicity. If I delay or fail to report Tom, I will be in violation of state regulations, and subject to citations and fines. I might also be in trouble with the medical board, as failure to report suspected TB— or measles, syphilis, chlamydia, meningitis, and forty-six other communicable diseases—is considered unprofessional conduct.

When the department of health gets my report, they start an investigation. A public health officer will visit Tom's dorm within three days to identify, examine, and evaluate his roommates.

What if Tom does not cooperate? What if he considers this to be his personal problem, or he can't handle it, or he just doesn't care? That's when the state steps in. There are "communicable disease laws"—these make the state responsible for preventing the spread of infectious diseases. If Tom does not show up for an appointment to be screened, examined, or treated, the public health nurse must reschedule him within a week. If he doesn't come to the second appointment, the public health nursing supervisor and the district public health investigator are notified. If Tom no-shows for his third appointment, he is served with a legal order to comply within seventy-two hours.

There's more. If Tom has TB, and there's reason to suspect that he is not taking his medications as directed, he may be required to have "directly observed therapy." That means the public health nurse will visit my patient twice a week for six months and watch him swallow his pills. If Tom remains uncooperative, and all alternatives have been exhausted, the state can detain him: he can, following due process, be confined in a locked facility. Justification for such an extreme measure? The protection of public health. Whether he likes it or not, the state sees to it that Tom is treated.

And they're right to do so. Because it's not just about Tom, whether he is ready to discover his condition, what he prefers or doesn't prefer. For the protection of public health against tuberculosis, the state has a long and strong arm. In addition to ordering Tom and his contacts to be screened, examined, treated, and detained, it can "isolate, inspect and disinfect persons, animals, houses, rooms, other property, places, cities, or localities." It can take possession of a corpse. It "may destroy such objects as bedding, carpets, household goods, furnishings, materials, clothing, or animals . . . when the property is in its judgment, an imminent menace to the public health."

I submit that my patient Brian is an imminent menace to the public health. I submit that for his welfare and the welfare of others, he and his contacts be required to be screened for HIV.

Why am I mandated to protect Tom, but not Brian? Why does the state send out public health officers in search of Tom's contacts, but not Brian's? Tom's roommates will be informed of their exposure; representatives from the deptartment of health will show up at their door and tell them all about it. Brian, if he ever gets around to asking, will just have to trust his boyfriend to tell the truth. And speaking of trust, I regret to inform you that when it comes to HIV, people lie.[6]

Come to think of it, if standard public health measures had been applied to the control of HIV, perhaps my patient might already have been tested and on drugs that might add years to his life. Isn't it worth the risk of feeling judged?

Brian and Tom are both potential victims, as well as carriers, of disease.[7] I am their physician, ostensibly responsible to the same degree for each of them. But look at the contrast: with Tom, the steps I follow are defined and enforced. For carelessness, I face citations and fines and my patient faces a court order. So Tom will be treated, and he'll be OK. But with Brian, I have no one to contact, no report to file. Brian can keep going like this for years, until he's able to "emotionally handle" bad news. And by then, the news may be *really* bad. In this country, HIV infection is generally discovered at an advanced stage, when treatment options are narrower, and in most cases less effective.[8]

An alien arriving on our planet and surveying the situation would conclude we care more about Tom and his friends than Brian and his. He'd be astonished to learn that this perplexing state of affairs is the result of gay activism during the early years of the epidemic. At the time, traditional public health measures, like mandatory reporting of cases by name and enforced partner notification, were seen by the gay community as an invasion of privacy; they waged a battle against public health officials, and they won.[9] Since then, HIV has had a special status among infectious diseases: voluntary and anonymous testing, no partner notification.[10]

More than twenty years later, this remains the case.[11] Welcome to the bizarre world of politically correct medicine, where I'm mandated to report Tom, but can only talk with Brian—without being offensive, of course. Add to this the PC message that "anybody can get HIV," the notion that it's an equal-opportunity virus, and what do you get? A scenario where high-risk Brian *underestimates* his danger,[12] and low-risk Sophia, whom you'll meet next, exaggerates hers.

CHAPTER V

Sophia's Meltdown

Sophia is frantic: her husband was unfaithful, and now she may have HIV. Even worse, she may have given it to her daughter, who is nursing. Sobbing loudly, she covers her face and rocks back and forth. I can only hand her tissues and wait.

Slowly, she's able to tell her story. Sophia is studying film, Ken is a dentist, and the baby is fourteen months old. Last week, while arguing, Ken told Sophia he's been with other women—she didn't ask how many, or when.

Since then, Sophia hasn't been able to eat, sleep, or concentrate. Driving to school yesterday, she rear-ended someone and was so upset she missed a class. Today it came to a head—Sophia was suddenly seized with terror, she was dizzy and short of breath, her hands shook, her heart pounded. What was it? An asthma attack? She didn't have asthma. A heart attack? But she's only twenty-six!

A friend took her to the emergency room. After blood work and an EKG, Sophia was told that the cause of her palpitations and hyperventilation was emotional: it had been a panic attack. The friend walked her to the campus counseling center, where an on-call therapist judged her distress and dysfunction to be severe enough for an emergency psychiatric evaluation—appointments usually reserved for suicidal or psychotic students.

I explore with Sophia what part of all this is most distressing to her. She is hurt by her husband's confession, and the marriage—troubled for years, and now in crisis—may not survive. But what's put her over the edge is the terror of HIV. This is Sophia's prime concern: her health, and the health of her baby. Everywhere she looks, it seems, is the warning "HIV is transmitted through bodily fluids: blood, semen, vaginal secretions, breast milk." When Sophia sees that, she's paralyzed with fright.

My first priority with this patient is to treat the anxiety that is interfering with her functioning. Sophia needs to be able to return to her jobs: mother and student (her wifely responsibilities have been put on hold). Because of fear of infection, Sophia has stopped nursing—in any case, her milk all but disappeared due to her stress—so I can safely prescribe a short trial of medication. This will help Sophia calm down, and to sleep, eat, and keep her panic at bay. She'll feel better in a day or two.

My plan is that during her next appointment, scheduled for later in the week, we can speak more about her health concerns, and I might assess to what degree she, her husband, and her child are at risk. This will be harder than giving her pills; I'll need to ask about some intimate matters that will make both of us feel awkward. So as I write the Ativan prescription for Sophia, and tell her how to use it, I'm aware that it's only partial treatment—the easy part.

In the meantime, I do some homework. Assuming the worst, that Ken had relations with an HIV-infected woman, how likely is it that he was infected, that he passed the virus to Sophia, and she to their daughter? How likely is this whole horrific scenario? I'm not sure. But if my patient is overestimating the ease of HIV transmission, the facts may reassure her, and I'd like to be able to provide them to her. Having access to a virtual library at my fingertips, with archives of hundreds of scientific and medical journals, it shouldn't be hard to sort this out.

In Sophia's drama, there are three routes of infection to consider: female to male, male to female, and mother to child. From the nearly universal warnings that "anyone can get HIV," one would conclude, as Sophia has, that the virus spreads in an equal-opportunity manner. But the first thing I learn from the medical literature is that the various routes of infection carry vastly different risks, and must be considered separately.

To begin, consider Ken and his female companions. Assuming he starts out uninfected,[1] how easy is it for him to get the virus from one of them?

There are two factors to consider. First, how common is HIV in women? Of the current living cases of AIDS[2] in my state through 2003, only 8 percent are women. The number of women with AIDS is less than a tenth of the number of women who have been diagnosed with cancer. So the chance of Ken meeting an infected woman is low: there just aren't that many of them around.

Second, how common is female-to-male transmission? This has been studied by looking at monogamous heterosexual couples in which the woman is infected, the man is not, and condom use is inconsistent. In one such study conducted over ten years, only two of eighty-two men were infected.[3] In an earlier, similar study, only one of seventy-two men was infected.[4] Of a total of almost 21,000 men with AIDS in New York City, in 1989, only eight were unequivocally infected by sexual transmission from a woman.[5]

It may be instructive for Sophia to hear about the first woman in the country known to have been infected with HIV.[6] Some call this an urban legend, but my source tells me it's valid.[7] She was a prostitute in San Francisco who used intravenous drugs. In 1977 she gave birth to a child, one of three, all of whom died of AIDS.[8] From before the birth of her first child until her death in 1987—a period of at least ten years—this woman was an active prostitute in the heart of the city's red-light district. If transmission from an infected woman to an uninfected man was a common event, many infected heterosexual men would have surfaced. But at that time, only two heterosexual men in San Francisco were infected.

Since the 1980s, HIV has remained concentrated in the same high-risk groups, at least in the United States. In public health surveillance reports, HIV and AIDS cases are placed in categories of "transmission risk factor," such as MSM (men who have sex with men), intravenous drug use, pregnancy, and so on. Under the "heterosexual" risk factor, the numbers often look high, sometimes up to 30 percent of the total number of cases. But look closely: *heterosexual* is defined in small print as including HIV/AIDS cases traced to sexual contact with bisexual men and drug users.

So it's unlikely Ken is HIV-positive—so unlikely that some would say the risk is close to zero. But for the sake of argument, let's say he is. How safe is Sophia? Here I must consider a delicate issue—their sexual behavior. HIV, like any self-respecting microbe, has one goal: to find a home and reproduce. And about this there is no doubt: the virus has an easier time doing this in the rectum than anywhere else.

It's not unusual for college women to have anal intercourse.[9] If Ken is HIV-positive, this behavior is dangerous; the studies confirming this are voluminous.[10] The reason is biology—actually, to be more precise, histology. Histology is the study of cells, what they do and how they are organized. This may be beyond what Sophia is capable of, or even interested in learning about, but to fully understand how HIV is transmitted, a comparison of the histology of the vagina with the histology of the rectum is mandatory.

For infection to occur, keep in mind that HIV must either enter the bloodstream or gain access to deeper tissues. This makes it a relatively difficult bug to pass along. Consider, for example, the highly contagious viruses that cause conjunctivitis.[11] They are easily transmitted on your finger, when you touch one eye and then the other. They can also live on inanimate surfaces, like towels or pillows, and infect you from there.

In contrast, for HIV to infect Sophia, it must reach a group of cells in her immune system referred to as "target cells." Only here can the virus make a home and reproduce. To reach target cells, the HIV must either bypass, or pass through, a barrier. For example, the addict sharing a dirty needle infects himself by injecting the virus directly into his bloodstream, bypassing the natural barrier, skin. The same is true for persons infected through blood transfusions. The infant nursed by an HIV-positive mother is infected when the virus passes through the lining of the digestive system. So the barrier is important to look at: it is the wall the virus must breach to succeed.

Assuming Sophia is healthy—without any STDs or conditions that would weaken her immunity—her vagina has some built-in properties that are protective from the get-go.[12] In fact, one of the functions of the vaginal lining is protection from infection.[13] The pH is low, which inactivates HIV.[14] Its mucus has anti-HIV proteins.[15] Its lining is twenty to forty-five cells thick, increasing the distance to be traversed by the virus.[16] Under the lining is a layer in which target cells are found; this area is rich in elastic fibers. Next is a layer of muscle, then more elastic fibers. This architecture allows for significant stretching of the vagina without tears or abrasions. Research has indicated that HIV is unable to reach target cells in the human vagina under normal circumstances.[17]

The rectum has a different structure. As part of the gastrointestinal system, it has a lining whose primary function is absorption, bringing in molecules of food and water. The pH is higher. Most important, the rectal lining—the barrier to be breached—is only one cell thick. Below that delicate lining are blood vessels and target cells. Elastic fibers are absent.

Early in the epidemic, it was assumed that fragility of the rectal barrier accounted for the more common male-to-male transmission. But later in the 1980s came a discovery: infection could occur *without* disruption of the barrier. Specialized cells on the rectal surface were able to latch on to the virus, take it in, and deliver it to target cells.[18]

M cells are abundant in a healthy human rectum.[19] Their function is to bring a sample of foreign, potentially dangerous particles for identification and response by the body's defense system. An M cell *wants* to attract microbes, so its surface is sticky, and it can fold over a virus or bacteria, engulf it, and bring it inside in a pocket.[20] The pocket moves to the other end of the M cell, to immune cells that process the microbe and determine the appropriate response: ignore it or rally against it.

Along comes HIV. It subverts the system, turning M cells into an express lane for invasion. The virus is packaged, transported, and handed over to immune cells that are one and the same as the target cells the virus must reach to cause disease. So M cells facilitate the virus's job. They FedEx HIV directly to a lymphocyte—delivery takes ten minutes.[21]

There are no M cells in the vagina. This is not to say transmission of HIV cannot happen there—it can. But for infection to occur, there must be some weakening of the system—an infection, bleeding, an open sore, trauma, cancerous cells.

For this and other reasons, some researchers argue convincingly that vaginal transmission is very rare.[22] They are supported by studies of prostitutes, averaging two to three hundred contacts a year, usually unprotected, in which AIDS was found only in women who were also intravenous drug abusers.[23] And keep in mind, this was in prostitutes, a population considered a reservoir of STDs, a risk factor for infection.

When a man gets HIV from a woman and passes it to another woman, the second woman is called a tertiary case.

Without tertiary transmission, there can be no epidemic. Because heterosexual tertiary transmission is so rare, the few cases that exist are famous.[24]

Should Sophia worry? It boils down to this: unless Ken's been sharing needles or spending time with a man, her chances of being HIV-positive are about 1 in 500 million.[25] And yes, that is less than the risk of her being hit by lightning.[26]

What a waste of a nervous breakdown! Poor Sophia is a wreck—and for what? She and her baby are fine. This week from hell happened only because everywhere my patient turns, she's fed distortions.

At the campus health center: "The following activities are considered risky for contracting HIV: Any sexual contact that includes the exchange of infected blood, semen, or vaginal secretions. . . . Any type of needle sharing . . . transfusions of blood . . ."

From a pamphlet at her gynecologist's office: "Infection with HIV is a serious threat to the health of women in the United States. . . . HIV infection is spread through contact with the body fluids of an infected person. This can happen during sex or by sharing needles used to inject drugs."[27]

From the CDC Web site:

> *These are the most common ways that HIV is transmitted from one person to another:*
>
> * *by having sex (anal, vaginal, or oral) with an HIV-infected person;*
> * *by sharing needles or injection equipment with an injection drug user who is infected with HIV; or*

• *from HIV-infected women to their babies before or during birth, or through breast-feeding after birth"*[28]

From the National Women's Health Network: "*HIV is colorblind.* It's contracted through unprotected sex—vaginal, oral, or anal—with an infected person. Someone can get HIV by sharing needles with someone who has it, and it can also be passed from an infected mother to her baby. Gay, bisexual, and straight people all get it. Black people, Latinos, and Asians. Young and old people get it. HIV does not discriminate.... *HIV is here to stay, and anybody can get it.* If you are sexually active or do drugs, it's a good idea to get tested."[29]

This is nuts! "Anybody can get it"? Lumping together a drug addict in a Bronx shooting gallery, a homosexual prostitute on Castro Street, and a coed and her first boyfriend? As if these three face the same risk, regardless of their behavior and whom they choose to do it with? One veteran AIDS researcher said, "It's as if we don't want to offend the tobacco companies, so we tell people—Lung cancer can be caused by radon, asbestos, tobacco, and air pollution." It's like advising people to get a chest X-ray if they've been exposed to anything on that list. You'd never see this, because 80 percent of lung cancers are related to tobacco.[30]

No wonder Sophia had a meltdown. No wonder she can't eat or sleep: the warning "Anybody can get it" is ringing in her ears. Luckily, I'll see Sophia soon and explain that she has exaggerated her risk. Other people aren't so lucky. They are so terrified they have AIDS they kill themselves.

A study of suicides in Finland during 1987 and 1988 revealed that twenty-eight were people with those concerns.[31] Many of them could identify the source of their worry— a recent sore throat, fatigue, loss of sleep or appetite— symptoms that had been publicized as warning signs in the intense AIDS information campaigns in the Finnish media. In two cases the trigger event was an AIDS-related television program. Most of the victims were depressed.[32] Many left notes expressing their belief that they had HIV and had infected their significant others. On autopsy, none was positive.

The authors conclude: "These figures probably underestimate the numbers. Fear of AIDS . . . is a problem triggered by the vast publicity given to AIDS-related symptoms in the mass media and by sexual guilt. . . . Health care personnel should bear in mind the potential effects of sensationalized and unbalanced reporting on health issues. AIDS in the 1980's may not have been the last media-boosted phenomenon to raise the fear of illness in vulnerable depressed people."

Well, of course the media is boosting our fears—the warning "Anybody can get it" is pushed at us relentlessly by the medical and public health establishment. "AIDS does not discriminate"? *Duh!* Of *course* it doesn't! It's bound by the laws of nature, not the EEOC! It's a *virus,* remember? HIV is more common in gays and drug addicts not because it's homophobic or racist, but because these groups have *behaviors* that put them at risk. It's *what* you do, and *whom* you choose to do it with. Is that so complicated a point to get across?

I guess it must be. And how did all this politics, sociology, and loaded rhetoric get into a discussion about a tiny bit of RNA, anyhow? The story was told in a Pulitzer Prize–winning article in the *Wall Street Journal*.[33]

In 1987, the CDC had a problem. Nearly all AIDS victims were homosexuals, bisexual men, drug addicts, and their girlfriends. Polls showed that most of America didn't see the disease as "their" problem, and some saw it as a punishment for immorality. There were fears of widespread housing and job discrimination. *Life* magazine had proclaimed on its cover, "Now No One Is Safe from AIDS," and Oprah had opined that one in five heteros would die of AIDS in the following three years.[34] Aside from that, the media wasn't too interested, and for sure Washington wasn't. But people were dying, and funds were needed for prevention and research. In some countries, AIDS seemed to have spread more easily among non-drug-using heterosexuals. CDC officials wondered, If Americans think the virus is someone else's problem, how sympathetic can they be toward the victims? And who will support funding? They hired a Madison Avenue advertising firm to help design a public relations campaign. An idea took form: present AIDS as an equal-opportunity virus. *That* would wake up America. They met, debated, and did some soul-searching. Their decision? The America Responds to AIDS campaign, in which the public would be bombarded with a terrifying message: Anyone can get AIDS.

A series of dramatic public service announcements were designed, featuring AIDS victims who looked like middle America. They were featured on television, radio, and print, in ads that were broadcast over and over in late 1987. A middle-aged, blond woman and the young son of a rural

Baptist minister looked at the camera and declared, "If *I* can get AIDS, *anyone* can." Omitted from the script: she had used intravenous drugs; he was gay.

Not everyone agreed with the plan. These public health professionals knew that the ads were misleading, but given their predicament, they decided it was worth it, thinking the campaign would do the most good in the long run.[35] The Left was happy—finally the nation would notice the plague that had hit gays hard. Stigma would decrease, and money would come. The Right was happy because the message would promote their "pro-family" agenda.

The problem is, it wasn't true. And twenty years later, it's still not true. In the United States, the great majority of HIV transmission can still be traced to high-risk behavior. When the surgeon general sent a four-page brochure out to 107 million households in 1988 with the warning that "Everyone is at risk," it was overstating the danger.[36] Is there harm in doing so?[37] Consider these points: first, the misappropriation of scarce health funds. Among women, the group at significant risk for infection is those who inject drugs, or whose partners do. These women also suffer from other diseases, poverty, and malnutrition. Wiser to send the money their way, instead of "educating" yuppie white women not at risk and urging them to be tested. Among men, many at high risk now believe there is nothing uniquely dangerous about their behavior, because after all, *everybody* is at risk. In fact, there is an unrealistic optimism in young men engaging in dangerous activities, among both the infected and the uninfected.[38]

"Anybody can get HIV"—perhaps technically correct, but profoundly misleading, because all the "anybodies" have widely varying risks of getting it, probably a million-fold differences.[39] The warning does more harm than good. Half the U.S. population has been tested for HIV, most of them like Sophia and Ken, but more than 300,000 other people, like Brian, are HIV-positive and don't know it.[40] To engage in high-risk behavior with multiple people, to have a false sense of optimism about being healthy, all the while being highly infectious—this constitutes a lethal combination for Brian, the gay community, and public health. To say nothing of the obvious: the public deserves to know the truth, especially from people whose salaries they pay.

This fiasco has been written about at length; as noted earlier, it was the topic of the 1996 *Wall Street Journal* article that won a Pulitzer Prize.[41] And ten years earlier, the intrepid *San Francisco Chronicle* journalist Randy Shilts explained,

> *nothing captured the attention of editors and news directors like the talk of widespread heterosexual transmission of AIDS. Such talk could be guaranteed air time and news space, which, in the AIDS business, quickly translated into funds and resources. Thus, even though epidemiological support for fears of a pandemic spread of AIDS among heterosexuals was scant, few researchers would say so aloud. There was no gain in taking such a position, even if it did ultimately prove to be honest and truthful."*[42]

So he wrote in his classic 1987 book *And the Band Played On*, which was called "a heroic work of journalism" by the *New York Times*.[43] Heroic it certainly was—the author bravely indicted persons large and small, from the White House down; anyone who in his opinion had failed to deal with the epidemic, because he considered it a "robust journalistic duty to tell the whole story."[44] But for his integrity he paid a price. For example, because Shilts dared to suggest that bathhouses—where one in eight patrons had syphilis or gonorrhea, and the average guest had 2.7 sexual encounters a night[45]—were breeding grounds for HIV, he was jeered and spat upon by radical gays.[46]

But for my young patients this is ancient history; they have never heard of Randy Shilts. And twenty years after his death from AIDS, the truths he exposed don't reach them either. Instead, the CDC's 1987 "Anybody can get it" campaign is etched in their brains, causing Sophia to have a meltdown, while guys like Brian don't even get tested. So why is the myth still with us? Because it serves a purpose: it supports the preposterous notion that male and female are the same, and their unions equivalent. It's a social agenda— don't believe it. Consider instead our anatomy, histology, and immunology. What spreads HIV is anal sex, shared needles, or a partner who does those things. If Randy Shilts were with us, that's what he'd want us to know. Isn't it time we forgot the Left and the Right, and just told it like it is?

CHAPTER VI

KELLY'S SUMMER VACATION

KELLY, NINETEEN YEARS OLD, JUST HAD AN ABORTION. SHE got pregnant during the summer, while traveling. Something must've happened to the condom.

The boy goes to school in Canada. They had known each other for a week when, at a party, the two of them drank too much. When Kelly got home, her period was late, but with everything she had to do—move, unpack, and decide on classes—there wasn't even a moment to think about it. Anyway, why should she worry? They had used protection. A few weeks passed; still no period. A nurse at the campus health center had this news: her uterus was enlarged; Kelly was seven weeks pregnant. Sure enough, the blood test was positive.

From that moment, Kelly told me, she was clear about how to proceed. Since she had no particular religious beliefs and believed wholeheartedly in a woman's right to choose, there was never any question for her. She phoned the boy, but he didn't say much; he sounded more shocked than she was. Calling back the following day, he said he'd support her decision; he wanted to send a check, he even offered to come be with her. But Kelly said no. Not that she couldn't use the money—she had to put the four hundred and fifty dollars on a credit card. And it wasn't that she didn't care for him—not at all. In fact, she explained, that's the worst part of this whole thing for her: she *did* like him, quite a lot. Before this awful mess, she had hoped to see him over Thanksgiving. But now everything between them was different; their relationship was so awkward and strained that it seemed unlikely that would happen. So, Kelly explained with sadness, it just felt better to handle it alone.

Kelly turned to Planned Parenthood, where she learned there were two kinds of abortions, surgical and medical, and that each had pros and cons. Overall, the counselor said, they were both very safe—many times safer than giving birth. Psychological problems afterward were rare, she explained, and most women felt relieved. Kelly decided to have the medical abortion, in which pills are taken to cause miscarriage. Even though it could take a few days, it would happen in the privacy of her apartment, and she'd have some degree of control over events. Now it's over. She feels relieved, but she also feels sad, guilty, and alone. Kelly would rather not speak to the boy, and she's at odds with her best friend. She'd been depressed before all this, and now she is more depressed. Could I prescribe some medication?

Before her psychiatric evaluation, Kelly had met with one of our psychologists. I pulled up her records on my computer: "This student is dealing with depression, feelings of loss and isolation," read the assessment, "as well as recovering from a recent medical problem." What? A "medical problem"? My first thought was, The therapist is protecting the student's confidentiality; my second, that the therapist perceived the abortion to be a minor event. Either way, it surprised me, and I made a mental note to find out what it was all about.

Now, all this was taking place in the days following Hurricane Katrina. As a provider of mental health services, I was bombarded with information about the anticipated psychological fallout of the disaster. Professional newsletters and Web sites were filled with grim predictions about expected rates of post-traumatic stress disorder, or PTSD, in survivors. Health-care professionals in every location were reminded of the importance of early diagnosis and treatment. They were urged to be on the lookout for "stress reactions": shock, anxiety, irritability, insomnia . . .

You might expect the target audience of this information campaign to have been limited to the survivors of the tragedy, but that would be incorrect. The American Psychological Association, for example, reached out to everyone—or at least, everyone who watches television: They warned on their Web site: Images of this catastrophe, even when viewed from far away, may cause feelings of "vulnerability."

On my campus, there was another angle: You may not have experienced this disaster firsthand, the counseling center's Web site pointed out, but you may be struggling with "issues highlighted in the aftermath of Katrina: inequity, race, social class, the inadequacy of our emergency preparedness and our institutional response." You may therefore feel frustrated, angry, and helpless, so we welcome you to join us in a series of meetings focused on Katrina, where you can "work through" your thoughts and feelings.

It seemed as if, following this hurricane, my colleagues in the mental health field were determined to find each and every individual experiencing even the slightest distress, and to reassure them: *your reactions are normal, your tears and insomnia expected. You are not alone. Here are tips that will help you get through the days ahead, numbers you can call and a Web site you can visit, and here's when you need to speak with a professional.* And to the credit of many government and social service organizations and individuals, it seemed they wouldn't stop until the job was done.

In my opinion, it was overkill, but it was well intentioned. We in mental health know that for some people, trauma will have profound consequences. We have seen how depression, fear, guilt, flashbacks, and irritability can interfere with daily life. We know too well the toll it can take on relationships, work, and physical health. Some survivors may turn to self-destructive behaviors in an effort to dull the pain: drug use, alcohol, gambling. Some will attempt suicide; a few will succeed. We know, too, that reactions to trauma may be complex. Psychogenic amnesia exists—that's when people don't recall details because doing so would overwhelm them. A soldier may survive the battlefield or a woman a rape, and initially appear to cope well. Only later—maybe years later—may they begin to dwell on what happened, to obsess and dream about it. Finally, we understand that as a person ages, earlier traumas will be reexamined and appraised from a new angle, depending on subsequent events: marriages, divorces, births, miscarriages, infertility, menopause, loss of loved ones.

Hurricanes and terrorist attacks make headlines; other traumas happen behind closed doors, and wounds are hidden due to shame and fear. This, we know, can be particularly destructive.

This is why psychology reaches out to survivors of trauma, because for many the process of speaking about it, sharing details, having an opportunity to openly grieve, mourn, question, and be angry, allows healing to begin. It's a process through which the victim should feel endorsed, and supported. Ideally, this work is done with others in the same position, people who have "been there." This can be enormously helpful, even lifesaving. And we need to identify the minority with more serious symptoms and bring them into the system for evaluation and treatment. It's a public health strategy, part of the ABCs of psychology.

Of course, not everyone who survives a traumatic event develops symptoms of a stress disorder. Most don't. But because we can't predict too well who will and who won't, we want to alert everyone, just in case, because when this occurs, it can be debilitating. It only makes sense.

That's why, when evaluating a new patient, we always consider the possibility of trauma or abuse in her past. If she has come in for ADD or Internet addiction, it makes no difference; we must ask: Have you been though any major trauma? Were you, or anyone in your family, the victim of sexual, physical, or emotional abuse? We do this because many people won't say unless specifically asked. And if we miss this portion of her history, it's a major oversight.

Now here's what I don't understand.

There are over a million abortions in the United States each year, and 52 percent are in women under twenty-five.[1] Most women having early abortions do not seem to have lasting emotional difficulties,[2] but many do. Even the study quoted by Planned Parenthood, in support of their statement that "most women do not experience psychological problems or regrets two years after their abortion"[3] indicates that after two years 28 percent of women reported more harm from the abortion than benefit, 19 percent would not make the same decision under the same circumstances, 20 percent were depressed, and 1 percent had post-traumatic stress disorder.[4] College campuses must be teeming with these women. The study also reported that younger age predicted a more negative response to induced abortion, and that with the passing of time, negative emotions like sadness and regret *increased,* and decision satisfaction *decreased.* That is, more women reported sadness and regret two years following an abortion than one month after the event.

Now, I don't know if Kelly will end up with long-term symptoms or not, but why is there an *assumption* she'll be fine? Why does student health not schedule a postabortion follow-up, to check on how she is coping?[5] Why are women like Kelly sent home from Planned Parenthood knowing what to do in case of fever or heavy bleeding, but without a number to call or a Web site to visit if she is distressed?[6] And why, if she is seen in the future at the campus counseling center, will she surely be asked whether she was ever beaten or neglected by her parents, but not if she ever had an abortion?[7]

Let's say for the sake of argument that we dismiss

the women with "only" sadness and regret, and consider a conservative estimate of 1 percent of women with post-traumatic stress disorder. Still, with over one million abortions annually, that's more than ten thousand women a year. Since the *Roe v. Wade* decision in 1973, that's a total of 420,000 women in the United States who may have PTSD related to abortion.[8]

Where are these women? Where do they go to talk? What number do they call, what Web site do they visit?

Some of them are logged on to afterabortion.com, "a neutral, non-political, non-religion based, non-judgmental place for women to communicate with each other after an abortion."[9] This is a remarkable site. Women from the United States, Canada, England, Ireland, Australia, Sweden, and elsewhere are here, providing to one another what psychology does not: a forum to share experiences, a place to find validation, support, and advice. "You can always come to this site," one member tells another, "because we are in different time zones. So when you need to talk, there's almost always someone, somewhere available." "Regardless of whether your abortion was 3 weeks ago, 3 years ago, or 30 years ago," the home page states, "you can find other women who understand."

It's a busy place: there are almost 90,000 threads, over 600,000 posts, and 1,000 new posts are added daily. There are chat rooms and on-line recovery groups. It's like a twenty-four-hour hotline, or a never-ending group therapy session. One of their rules: no discussion about politics or morality.

One support board is for women who are seriously grieving: "Here you can discuss the intense feelings of loss, regret and despair that linger when you have an abortion and later either regret it or are feeling haunted by the what-ifs." The thread titles are filled with urgency: "Need help—NOW!!!"; "I'm losing it . . ."; "Suffocating"; "Can't breathe"; "Tears won't stop"; "Oh man can it get any worse?"; "Sad Scared Alone"; "Breakdown"; "Someone please please help"; "Numb"; "Why??????????"; "Can't do this anymore." It goes on and on; there are over seventeen hundred threads here.

PTSD is diagnosed when specific symptoms are present following an intensely distressing event. Typically, the traumatizing event is military combat, rape, assault, kidnapping, an accident, a natural disaster, war, or torture. But it could also involve seeing someone severely injured or killed. The immediate response involves intense fear, helplessness, or horror.

Following the event, some—but not all—people reexperience it in dreams, flashbacks, or on the incident's anniversary. The reexperiencing causes severe distress. Some victims feel numb, detached from reality and other people. They may not be able to recall details of the event, or they may be unable to forget them. Some will avoid thoughts, activities, or places that remind them of the event. They may be excessively moody or angry, overly sensitive, and unable to sleep or concentrate. When a survivor of a traumatic event has suffered for at least one month with reexperiencing, avoidance of stimuli, and hyperarousal, she qualifies for a diagnosis of post-traumatic stress disorder. When these symptoms occur following an abortion, some have called the condition post-abortion stress syndrome (PASS).[10]

Many women on afteraborti on.com write about the people, places, or things that remind them of their abortion, causing deep pain; these are "triggers." Sensitive to the need of members to share experiences, but mindful of the possibility their entries will cause distress to others, the site uses "trigger warnings." Members are advised:

> *A trigger warning serves as a heads up that the post contains some possibly upsetting material. Triggery subjects include, but are not limited to, pregnant women, children, clinic protestors, insensitive people . . . anniversaries, etc. Many of the ladies (and guys!) here are feeling down and can be easily upset. Trigger warnings are advanced warning NOT to read if you're feeling sensitive or easily upset. If you feel your post may be upsetting to others, you may add a trigger warning. On occasion a moderator may add one for you, if they determine that it's necessary.*

Reading the board on triggers provides a glimpse of the agony that an ordinary day can bring some women who have had abortions. Maternity stores, baby clothing, strollers, and cribs; kittens, puppies, a pregnant friend, a child calling "Mommy"; the abortion date, the due date, Mother's Day; a happy family, a kite, a song, biology class, a museum exhibit, a pro-life demonstration, a bumper sticker, menstruation, the sound of a vacuum cleaner. Many are young women in high school or college. They describe being "triggered" by a movie or TV show they are watching with their parents or boyfriend, and having to hide their sorrow and rage. No wonder they log on to this site—to find an international sisterhood, company for their misery.

And they really are there for each other—listening, soothing, and sending hugs. Here's how they sound: "Yes, I too had the same thing, same vision, same, same, same. . . . O hun, I can see why that is so upsetting. . . . You have every right to feel upset and angry. . . . I can totally relate . . . yep, me too!! Horrible isn't it? . . . The only advice I can give is chocolate. Lots and lots of chocolate . . . my heart is with you. . . . Oh sweetie, I am so sorry for what you are going thru, I'd be crying too. . . . PM or email me anytime . . . (((((hugs))))) . . . I hope you are OK . . . You poor thing. But you are strong and we are all here for you. . . . Hang in there, ok? . . . I've noticed that drinking warm milk when I'm really upset sometimes helps to calm me down. . . ."

For anyone still wondering how an abortion might, for *some,* fall into the category of a traumatic event, read on. But be advised, the material you are about to read has been given a "trigger warning." It will be difficult to absorb, even for those who are not survivors of trauma.

The following phrases are from a message board whose topic is medical abortion, the kind Kelly had. Posting here are women who saw a fetus in the blood clots and tissues they passed—a tiny head, the beginnings of arms and legs. They had not been warned of this possibility beforehand. Listen to them speak: "It's been a year and a half, but I can still remember how it looked and felt. . . . I held my baby in my hand . . . white, like mucus I thought at first until I looked closer and my mind accepted what I was seeing. Head, eyes, nose, arms, fingers . . . I cried over it,

kissed it . . . *sigh* that was the worst part of all . . . I remember seeing the embryo . . . clear as day, I knew what
she was. I couldn't fool myself. I stared at her for the
longest time . . . felt like eternity. I will never forget that
sight as long as I live. . . ."

"I saw every little feature perfectly . . . it was very, very
tiny . . . just stared at it. . . . was in shock . . . shut off my
thinking . . . it was surreal . . . like I was trapped in a horror movie . . . can't lose the image . . . won't stop replaying
in my mind . . . haunting me . . . horrifying . . . reminded
every day . . . it's what I see when I go to bed . . . can never
un-see what I saw . . . see it every day in my mind . . . can't
lose the image . . . don't know how to deal with this . . .
haven't told anybody . . . horrifying . . . nightmares . . . lots
of nightmares . . ."

One woman wrote, "I can't even believe I'm typing
these words." And *I* couldn't believe I was *reading* them:
ghastly accounts of seeing the fetus and not knowing what
to do. "I had to dispose of it myself and I couldn't think of
anywhere to bury it that I could be sure an animal wouldn't
dig it up . . . didn't know what to do . . . should I save it . . .
bury it . . . flush it . . . didn't want to flush it, . . . couldn't
think of what else to do . . . was so horrified, I couldn't
move . . . I was guiltridden for years about putting it in the
toilet, but I didn't know what else to do . . . wish someone
had said there was a chance I would see it clearly and that I
should prepare myself for what I was going to do . . . left
mine in a cardboard dish . . . wrapped her in a piece of tissue and put her in the bedpan . . . wish I'd taken her and
buried her properly . . . wish I would have buried mine,

but I was too young and too stupid . . . if only . . . can't forget just flushing my baby away . . . I will never forgive myself for this, never ever . . ."

As a psychiatrist, what do I learn from this Web site? First, I see in these women what I see in many of my patients—exceptional strength and courage. They continue to function, even with their hideous flashbacks and raw emotions. Somehow they go to school and work, cook meals, drive carpool. To me, they are heroines, no less than anyone else who gets up each day with a broken spirit and heart and finds a way to survive.

Second, many women here have textbook cases of PTSD. Some have severe cases, and would benefit from therapy and medication. A few are hopeless and suicidal, and sound to me to be in need of hospitalization.

It's disturbing that these women are neglected by mainstream mental health. I am dismayed to learn they have nowhere to turn but a Web site. I am alarmed that girls and women being prepared for abortion are left unaware of the possible scenarios ahead of them. It's fine to reassure that the majority will do OK, but since when, in medicine, do we omit giving a heads-up regarding worst-case scenarios, however unusual? When I prescribe a medication with a one-in-a-thousand chance of causing a dangerous rash, my patient must be made aware of the risk. Isn't it a matter of informed consent?

I remind you that most of the million abortions performed each year are on single women under the age of twenty-five.[11] It's bad enough that we have no campus outreach to them, like we do for victims of abuse or date rape. What's worse is when one of these women does walk through our doors for help with depression, an eating disorder, or insomnia, we don't routinely ask, "Have you ever been pregnant?" and we're satisfied to assume her symptoms are due to other stressors in her life: school, finances, conflict with parents.

The woman herself may not know—or want to know—the source of her pain: she may genuinely believe her symptoms "came out of nowhere." Didn't everyone say that following the abortion she'll feel relieved, that the sadness will be short-lived, that there are essentially no long-lasting effects? If there are others like her, where are the posters and fliers on campus, affirming her feelings and listing times and locations of support groups? And finally, if she sought help at the counseling center and the professional with a degree *didn't even ask about it,* doesn't all this support her denial: My crying spells, insomnia, and falling grades aren't related to my abortion . . . right?

"I meet young women who dissolve into tears at the mention of a previous abortion," wrote a women's-health nurse for students at a large urban university.[12] In her article "The 'A' Word," she described how her patients felt so stigmatized and traumatized that they couldn't even *say* "abortion." Of course, *she* bothered to ask—as a nurse, it's routine. So why isn't it for campus therapists?

Because it's not politically correct. Campus counseling doesn't want to take the risk of suggesting that abortion can be traumatic—that's a word reserved for victims of rape, abuse, harassment, or natural disasters. So while everyone is bewildered at the mental health crisis on our campuses, not one voice suggests that perhaps the aftermath of abortion contributes to the staggering statistics. I see no attention given to the topic in the journal or annual meetings of the American College Health Association, or in the book out of Harvard mentioned earlier about the campus mental health crisis.[13] Neither do I find "The 'A' Word" anywhere on the American Psychiatric Association's Web site focused on college mental health issues.[14]

One woman, who was shocked at the lack of "emotional aftercare" following her abortion, put it well: "When I got my abortion, I was really mad at the feminists. You gave me this choice—great! But then I'm on my own afterwards? What's up with that?" A coordinator of a Reproductive Rights Action League explained, "There have been moments where the movement has been scared to say that abortion may have emotional effects."[15]

Moments? What an understatement! In nearly every medical, mental health, and women's health organization, the denial of the trauma of abortion is entrenched dogma: the experience is just not that big a deal.[16]

Shock, denial, numbness, distressing memories, flashbacks, avoidance, irritability, poor concentration, nightmares? These don't occur following abortion. So concluded a psychologist involved in the study done by Surgeon General Koop on the health effects of abortion, at the request of President Reagan. "We searched and searched and searched," he said, and there was "no evidence at all for the existence of the 'postabortion syndrome' claimed by some right-to-life groups."[17] The surgeon general himself may have seen it differently: in a letter to the president he stated that most of the research was "flawed," that there was insufficient evidence to draw conclusions, and that more research was needed.[18]

"The best studies available on psychological responses to unwanted pregnancy terminated by abortion in the United States," concluded a landmark *American Psychologist* article, "suggest that severe negative reactions are rare, and they parallel those following other normal life stresses. The time of greatest distress is likely to be before the abortion . . . abortion is usually psychologically benign."[19]

Planned Parenthood considers symptoms of trauma following abortion a "non-existent phenomenon" circulated by "anti-family planning extremists."[20] They quote psychological research to support their belief that abortion is "a positive coping mechanism": "For most women who have had abortions, the procedure represents a maturing experience, a successful coping with a personal crisis situation. . . . Women who have had one abortion do not suffer psychological effects. In fact, as a group, they have higher self-esteem, greater feelings of worth and capableness, and fewer feelings of failure than do women who have had no abortions." On a Web site for teens, Planned Parenthood explains, "Abortion is a very safe procedure. It's about twice as safe as having tonsils removed."[21]

The American Psychiatric Association agrees. Introducing an article entitled "The Myth of the Abortion Trauma Syndrome," a vice president of that group began, "This is an article about a medical syndrome that does not exist."[22] She argued that while women may experience an abortion as a loss, and thus feel sad afterward, a feeling is "not equivalent to a disease," and that transient feelings of stress and sadness should be distinguished from psychiatric illness.

It doesn't sound to me like the girls and women posting on afterabortion.com are experiencing "transient feelings of stress and sadness." It sounds to me like they are falling apart. Even Hillary Clinton, on the anniversary of *Roe v. Wade*, said abortions are a "sad, even tragic choice to many, many women."[23] Does she know something that the American Psychological Association and Planned Parenthood don't?

It's worth recalling at this point that PTSD itself was conceived in more of a sociopolitical climate than a medical one. In its infancy, it was considered by some in psychiatry an unfounded diagnosis, arbitrarily making the normal reactions of soldiers returning from combat into a mental disorder.[24] And since its official recognition by psychiatry in 1980, the definition of PTSD has been continuously redefined and broadened, so that currently many more people now qualify for the diagnosis, not fewer.

PTSD was first defined as resulting from an event that "would evoke significant symptoms of distress in most people, and is generally outside the range of usual human experience."[25]

In 1994, the criteria for PTSD were loosened. The event didn't have to be "outside the range of usual human experience." Instead, it just had to be "traumatic."[26] With that adjustment, the prevalence of PTSD automatically increased; some mental health professionals questioned this process.[27]

The broadening continued. The event that originally had to be "outside the range of usual human experience" has come to include many types of widespread occurrences. As a result, the terms *trauma, distress, horror,* are watered down. Thus one report argues that victims of sexual harassment may meet diagnostic criteria for PTSD, and another claims that it is found in gynecological patients due to "insensitive obstetric care" or "hostility on the part of clinical staff."[28] When it comes to horrors, that's a long way from My Lai and Auschwitz.

Given the watering down of PTSD and the trend toward including more and more victims under its tent, it is all the more surprising that psychology refuses to acknowledge the trauma—the *real* trauma—of abortion to some women. With therapists reaching out to victims of every sort of natural and man-made disaster, child abuse, bullying, harassment, domestic violence, and boorish gynecologists, how can it be deaf to the anguish of tens of thousands of women, wounded and grieving, who huddle together in cyberspace?[29]

Jilly says it's about politics and money. She's afterabortion. com's creator and owner, "a prochoice woman," as she describes herself, "who believes abortion should remain legal." But Jilly also believes in PASS, because, she writes, "I have experienced it myself." Jilly has done her homework, and knows what she's talking about.

She compares PASS with two other emotional conditions unique to women: postpartum depression and premenstrual dysphoric disorder (more commonly known as PMS). Both are officially recognized as serious health issues, with pharmaceutical companies eager to fund research and conferences. Women with these diagnoses get support and medication, and their insurance pays for it. Jilly explains:

> There is nothing political about postpartum depression or a menstrual period. Every woman, Christian, atheist, prochoice, prolife, gets their period. And a prochoicer wouldn't complain about women getting treated for postpartum depression, or say that it hurts the cause of women's freedom of choice. A prolifer would not use postpartum depression as a way to try and discourage childbirth, and say that childbirth or menstruation "hurts" women, or that childbirth is "killing" women. . . . Those issues are non-political women's health issues. There's no "bad side" to be on with these problems.
>
> . . . With post-abortion stress syndrome, it's very different. If a woman suffers from PASS . . . the concern for her actual health problem disappears, and she becomes a pawn in the rhetoric of the abortion war. She gets no official treatment or support. . . . She gets told what she is experiencing does not exist, or "only happens to women with previous psychological problems."

There's no medical research done on PASS, Jilly goes on, because there are no grants from pharmaceutical companies.

> The drug companies that fund medical research that allows a disorder to be diagnosed and "medically accepted" will not go anywhere near research for PASS. Why? Because they don't want to touch the political suicide that anything related to abortion is. . . . Why jeopardize the

*profitability of all their base drugs by looking into some-
thing controversial that may bring them protests and
boycotts from both sides of the abortion war, regardless of
how their research turns out?*

*... The prochoice majority says PASS "does not ex-
ist" and that antiabortionists are using it to try and scare
women away from abortion, and to try and influence
lawmakers that abortion is dangerous. The prolifers agree
that PASS exists, but they use it (as the prochoicers fear)
as a way to discourage abortion, and as a way to help re-
voke abortion rights. The woman who is suffering is left
alone as the two sides argue, and the medical community
stays out of it.*

I couldn't have said it better myself. The medical community *is* staying out of it, despite evidence supporting
Jilly's position.[30] And the women who are suffering pay the
price—victims a second time.

Getting back to Kelly, what can we say at this early
point about how the abortion will affect her in the future?
She has a history of depression and no social support: these
place her at some risk for long-term problems. On the
positive side, she had clarity about her decision—no apparent confusion or mixed feelings—and the abortion did not
go against her beliefs. She made the decision indepen-
dently and was able to choose when and where it would
happen. And what may be most important, she now recog-
nizes her distress and has come for help.

But there is someone overlooked in this discussion, an
essential participant in this drama, who is strangely anonymous and peripheral: "the boy."

From the little I know of him, and excusing his behavior while intoxicated, he sounds like a decent person. He took responsibility, offered to pay, and even volunteered to come be with Kelly during the difficult time. Sounds like this was a significant event for him, and I wonder—how is *he* coping? What are *his* thoughts and feelings? What are his background and beliefs? Who is he talking to?

Now that I think about it, what's it like for *any* boy or man? How does it feel to be told: I conceived with you, and now I'm getting an abortion—this is just to let you know. What's it like to have someone else—sometimes someone you barely know and may never see again—decide the fate of a clump of cells that could become your child?

This is an overlooked subject: the *man's* response to abortion. Forget about psychology's denial of women's negative reactions—at least they *consider* the possibility. But the emotional reactions of *men* to abortion? It's not even on the radar screen.[31]

A search of the subjects "men" and "abortion" on the social sciences database on psychINFO produced thirty documents. Eleven of these addressed the topic of men's reactions to their partner's abortions; the others focused on other issues such as attitudes and decision making. Compare that with the number of documents about "bullying": 1413; "harassment": 3522; "multiculturalism": 2277; and "abuse": 47,129. As with the nameless young man in Kelly's tale, we just don't know what the story is with the hundreds of thousands of boys and men involved in an abortion each year.

There is only one academic nonpartisan book devoted exclusively to this topic.[32] It didn't come from the mental health field; it was written by a sociologist and a poet/

writer, both male "abortion vets," both ardently prochoice, who wanted to understand "this confusing and troubling experience—perhaps the least well known and least understood of any challenges in a man's life." In their own words:

> *Looking back on it now, I recognize I had been little prepared for the complex reality of an abortion. . . . Because I was very upset by my partner's fright and bewilderment, I had rushed to assure her of my total support. But in the process, I had rushed right past the task of gaining any insight into my own confused feelings and ideas. (Arthur Shostak)*

> *I have explored the world of abortion enough to know that men are seriously affected by their abortion experiences and that their memories are extremely sharp and cogent. . . . Although there are a variety of social-political responses to the subject of abortion in America, I have been most impressed by the lack of response to the often forgotten partner. . . . Like many men . . . I chose to get my abortion experience behind me. I failed. (Gary McLouth)*

These two, motivated by the memory of their own ordeals, studied a thousand boys and men whose girlfriends, fiancées, or wives were having abortions.[33] The men completed a 102-item questionnaire while in the waiting rooms of thirty abortion clinics around the country. The results indicated that many, if not most, men seated in those waiting rooms were quietly enduring considerable pain and turmoil: 80 percent thought either "occasionally" or "frequently" about the child that would not be born; 47 percent agreed with the statement, "Males involved in an abortion have disturbing thoughts about it afterwards"; 91 percent would have liked to join their partner in the recovery room; 75 percent of men had talked to no one about the crisis other than their partner; 74 percent were interested in some form of counseling; 54 percent would have liked a group session with other men; and 91 percent "were emphatic about their desire never again to be in this situation."[34]

"Little wonder," one of the authors concluded, "that 80% of the 1000 males referred to their vigil as the longest, hardest half day of their lives . . . an encounter, never forgotten, with that 'dark involvement with blood and birth and death.' "[35]

The same authors surveyed seventy-five men whose abortions had been months or years earlier. So much for the belief that time heals all wounds. Whereas only 3 percent of waiting-room men thought the abortion would contribute to the breakup of their relationship, 25 percent of the postabortion men thought it had. The 47 percent who thought that day that they'd have disturbing thoughts afterward? With time, the number of men with those thoughts was 16 percent higher. Overall, an astonishing 60 percent of men described still having occasional thoughts about the fetus: "We heard, over and over again, of day and night dreams of the child that wasn't born, and about fantasies of their adequacy as new fathers—though all emphasized the effort they made to consciously control these mental maladventures."

Some believe that men are at *greater* risk than women

after an abortion. They point out that men more often blame the unwanted pregnancy on their own character, leading to more guilt and depression.[36] They mention the social sanctions against male grieving, and the tendency of boys and men to react with denial and distancing, instead of asking for help. There is also the perception of being helpless, with nothing to do, and of abortion clinics ignoring them and their needs. Add to that the difficulty many males have dealing with intense emotional situations, the pressure to appear strong, the desire to focus on their partner's needs, and the secrecy and isolation, and you have the makings of a burden too heavy for most mature adults to bear, let alone those still on their way.

Other studies support the findings that some men experience significant suffering after an abortion, and recommend that boys and men be included in abortion center counseling.[37] A *Los Angeles Times* survey found more regret and guilt among postabortion men than postabortion women, and half the calls to a postabortion counseling hotline in the Bay area are from men.[38]

Here's what it was like for the sociologist researcher to interview some of these postabortion men:

> *Scores of males ... have told me I was the first person they had ever told of their part in an abortion months or even years before. Many cried with the relief disclosure and processing makes possible. We would sit in the back of a dinner [sic] in a booth I had "reserved" for an hour's interview, and still be there hours later, with crumbled Kleenex tissues strewn about, and a sympathetic waitress hovering nearby to keep the coffee cups filled.*[39]

It would appear reasonable to suggest that for some men, abortion leaves scars. And with an average of one million abortions a year, even small percentages—and the limited data we have suggests they may not be that small—translate into a considerable mass. But what hope do these men have, if postabortion women with full-blown PTSD don't exist for the mental health field?

Will someone please explain to me, why does psychology, in its quest to identify and counsel every victim of possible child abuse, sexual harassment, or hurricanes,[40] leave no stone unturned, and then go berserk at the suggestion that maybe, *maybe,* some—not all, but *some*—women and men hurt for a long, long time after abortion, and they too need our help?[41] Will someone help me understand why seeing your home destroyed by water automatically places you at risk for a psychiatric disorder, but having your pregnant uterus emptied "by gentle suction,"[42] or flushing your fetus down the toilet, well, that brings relief?

I'll tell you why. Because it's not politically correct to consider abortion to be more than a medical procedure: the removal of "tissue" or of "uterine contents." If some people hurt following abortion, if women can get PTSD and men mourn silently for years, then that means sometimes it's bad, like war or hurricanes. And if you are in the mental health profession and want to keep your job, you'd better think long and hard before you say *that.*

Were it not so necessary for psychology to remain politically correct, the emotional fallout of abortion might be seen differently. In Japan, abortion is a social necessity and a relatively noncontroversial issue.[43] It is not a private choice that is either right or wrong, but a responsible, practical decision made with the well-being of the nation in mind.

Buddhist folklore holds that the soul of a fetus lives in a kind of purgatory where it is unable to be reborn.[44] Parents can save it through *mizuko kuyo,* a ritual in which the fetus is memorialized. It's a popular thing in Japan, and you'll see simple shrines erected by the side of a road, as well as elaborate, expensive ceremonies in temples. You might also see the statue of Jizo, the guardian of aborted fetuses, placed on an altar in private homes.

Ceremonies in temples are public affairs. Whole families come, register, and pay for the service, which is performed by Buddhist priests and takes about forty-five minutes. Everyone recites these verses, presumably what the fetus would say if it could:

> *I was invited [in]to [the] lives of Father and Mother,*
> *Lived within Mother's womb for days and months,*
> *During the time that I was continuing to grow,*
> *I had requested the kindness of my parents,*
> *I disobeyed that kindness,*
> *So I was brought out by the midwife with the body lost*
> *Father help me and mother help me too.*
> *Help give the soul, whose power is limited and voice*
> *   cannot speak*
> *In order to not become a soul lost in the darkness.*[45]

The abbot explains to the families how the ritual helps the soul of the fetus and exonerates the guilt of "those who come with heavy heart of regret and ambivalence." A study of over a thousand participants of *mizuko kuyo* found that some of them had been performing the ritual for over thirty years. Some Japanese medical professionals now acknowledge the possibility that abortion may cause grief—a recognition that has not been met with controversy.

Psychology can learn from this. Our culture is stuck in a rigid, polarized view of abortion and its aftermath. It's either right, without victims or fallout, or it's wrong. It's either constitutional or it's unconstitutional. This works at church or in court, but not in my line of work. People are more complicated than ideology, and psychotherapists are supposed to know that. The inner life is a fluid tangle of wounds and fears, longings and dreams. A pregnancy is a new, enormous relationship,[46] if only a potential one: I could now be a mother, a father; and an abortion is the decision to end that relationship, that possibility. These are tremendously profound and complex issues for women and men. To suggest that pregnancy and abortion do not touch essential parts of us is to deny our depth and sensitivity, and to diminish the awe and magnitude of creating a child. To compare an abortion with a tonsillectomy—as a procedure you go in for, take a Tylenol, and get on with your life—is a hideous defamation of us all.

We see that when politics and ideology are removed from this debate, as in Japan, the needs of postabortion men and women can surface and be acknowledged. Healing can begin. What appear to be two contradictory truths can be grasped, without one denying the legitimacy of the other. The same abortion may bring relief *and* lasting pain. The decision that seemed best in college may be perceived as tragic at menopause. It is our job in psychology to provide—how did Jilly describe her Web site?—a neutral place of healing. How can we do that, when the profession is aligned ideologically with one side, and makes pronouncements like "abortion is for the most part benign"? How will patients see therapists as neutral when even our definitions of "trauma" and "horror" must be politically correct? One can only imagine how it feels, for a woman harrowed by flashbacks of fetal parts, to learn that mental health experts consider her experience "nonexistent."

Our job is not to proclaim whether abortion is good or bad; our job is to ask, and listen. Let our patients come and tell *us* what abortion has been like *for them*.

If psychology were truly concerned with all victims, not only those that advance their ideological agendas, their outreach would include individuals traumatized by abortion. The APA would acknowledge these men and women, and deplore their revictimization by agenda-driven groups who render them invisible. It would enthusiastically promote new treatment techniques, drawn from the ancient wisdom of Buddhism and the ritual of *mizuko kuyo*. Enterprising psychotherapists would import statues of Jizo, and patients would set up altars where they could express regret and ask forgiveness. Professional mental health organizations would insist that commercial abortion providers, who make sizable profits, provide comprehensive counseling before and after their services. It would make sure that a diagnostic category exists in the *Diagnostic and Statistical Manual of Mental Disorders* that describes their condition, for legal and insurance purposes.

And finally, it would caution every psychologist, psychiatrist, or social worker to fully explore the abortion question when evaluating any patient, male and female, lest they risk underestimating—or missing altogether—what for some is an open wound, a wound as bad, maybe worse, than the memory of a hurricane.

CHAPTER VII

───────

Delia's Dream

Meet Delia—pretty, dynamic, and ambitious. She was diagnosed with attention deficit disorder as a child, and comes in a few times a year for Ritalin refills. At twenty-seven, she is about to get her Ph.D. in geology. Delia has a great job lined up in Dallas, and can't wait to shine there. We speak about life after graduation and her long-term goals. She wants to establish her career, pay back loans, and get married. What about kids? I ask. Oh, yes, for sure, she says with a smile, I've always known I wanted kids. My dream is to have three or four. And, Delia adds, fertility won't be a problem, because in college she unfortunately had to get an abortion. So there are no worries in that area.

Delia's enthusiasm is infectious, with her easy smile and positive attitude. Her future looks bright indeed. I share her excitement about all the good things yet to come, congratulate her on her accomplishments, and urge her to keep in touch.

She leaves, and I review her records. The treatment for ADD has been straightforward, and does not concern me. But her women's health history has red flags.

Sexually active at sixteen, one STD, one abortion, on the pill for seven years, eleven lifetime male partners.

Nothing that unusual—her history is like that of many of her peers. Still, Delia's sexual lifestyle puts her at risk for some problems when she decides to start her family. The reason: an infection treated long ago, so long it's nearly forgotten—chlamydia.

At the time, Delia took antibiotics for a week, as did her boyfriend. Testing negative a few months later, they were pronounced cured. No infection, clean as a whistle, like it never happened. Another miracle cure, thanks to antibiotics? The current experts say . . . maybe.

My medical school text, published the year Delia was born, describes *Chlamydia trachomatis* as a cause of blindness in third-world countries, spread by dirty fingers and flies.[1] Only secondarily does it mention the bacteria as a venereal disease, as sexually transmitted diseases were called then. By the time Delia was a teen, chlamydia was gaining ground as an STD. Now it's the most common sexually transmitted bacteria, responsible for three million new cases a year in the United States, most of them in young women.

Yes, that's *three million new cases a year.* The yearly cost of managing chlamydia and its consequences: $2.4 billion.

It's a clever little bug.[2] It sneaks into a healthy cell, hides out, pilfers food, and multiplies. It evades detection in the most ingenious ways, for instance, by wrapping itself in molecules stolen from the host's own skin, fooling the cell into thinking it belongs there. The chlamydia outsmarts its host, who is blind to the enemy within until the end.

When the body gets wind of the attack, it reacts with

inflammation. White cells and chemical messengers arrive to contain the invasion by walling it off. There is swelling and heat, but usually too little to cause pain or fever. Normal tissue is damaged, and in healing forms a scar. That's not usually a big deal, unless the scar is in a structure with a tiny canal, like the fallopian tubes.

You see, in a woman, chlamydia starts in the lower genital tract, with infection of the opening of the uterus. That's not so dangerous; there are other organisms there, and the vagina has a pretty effective self-cleaning system. But sometimes the bugs travel quietly through the cervix, perhaps by hitching a ride on a sperm going that way. They reach the uterus and then settle down in the fallopian tubes, areas that are normally sterile. The diameter of the tubes is about one millimeter. As they are so narrow, it doesn't take much of a scar to block or even seal them closed. Scarred tubes cause ectopic pregnancy—which can kill—and fertility problems.

About four inches long, the fallopian tubes retrieve the egg from the ovary and carry it toward the uterus. It's worthwhile spending a moment describing the remarkable way this happens.[3]

It's like a complex dance, or a symphony. There are players, choreography, movement, rhythm, a beginning and an end. Instead of ballerinas and a wind section, there are specialized cells and messengers in the blood. They have dry, lifeless names—columnar epithelium, endosalpinx, prostaglandin F2a—that belie their mystery and wonder.

Every month, a message from the brain to the fallopian tubes says: Get ready—an egg is on the way. Drop down to the ovary, sweep its surface, and find the ovum about to be released. Contract your muscles and lift up the egg. Rev up the cilia, the tiny hairs; pull in the prize with their current. Make juice, and make it rich—then nourish the egg, and watch it grow. Now relax your muscles, float the egg downstream, and prepare for the big moment: fertilization.

For all this to go off without a hitch requires precise timing and coordination, exact levels of hormones, and exquisitely sensitive cells. And so it is: a weak message from the brain—no ovum matures. Cilia beating out of sync—the egg is lost. Fluid gone awry—it starves. A canal too wide will rush it, but in a narrowed one, the egg may get stuck. Estrogen low when you need it, or high when you don't, and the whole operation is out of whack. A million things could go wrong in that four-inch area.

Did Delia's infection reach her tubes? There's no way to know now, without doing invasive tests. It's possible she was treated early, before the bacteria had a chance to travel. That's the best scenario: the bacteria are gone, and her tubes are wide open.

But what's "early"? Time is of the essence in treating chlamydia; we're in a race to get it before it advances. Once it reaches the tubes, it may be impossible to eradicate.[4] Sexually active women who show up for their yearly checkups should be routinely screened for chlamydia, and treated if positive. But what if they were infected months earlier? How long does it take for the bacteria to reach the tubes? We don't know. In the female pig-tailed macaque monkey, it takes about eight weeks.[5]

There's more we don't know. We don't know, for one thing, how well the screening test identifies cases where the infection is dormant. A negative result does not guarantee the absence of infection.[6] We're not sure which antibiotic is best, or how long treatment should last. We don't know if treatment always wipes out the whole infection. It's possible that in some cases, medication temporarily stops the bacteria from reproducing, only to be reactivated later.[7] And we don't understand why women with chlamydia are more likely to get cervical cancer.

We *do* know that most women who have been infected discover it in a startling way—when they can't conceive. Since in up to 80 percent of infected women, chlamydia produces no pain, fever, or discharge, a woman thinks she's fine. Like her infected cells, she's an unsuspecting hostess to a dangerous guest. Years later, when she's settled down, married, and put the partying and hookups behind her, she's told that her blood has antichlamydial antibodies— evidence of old infection. The doctor puts a scope through her navel to look at her fallopian tubes, and discovers they are enlarged and scarred by adhesions. And this is the reason she cannot have a baby.

The experts say that Delia may hear this someday, because she has some of the risk factors that may lead to chlamydia infection: intercourse at an early age, many partners, and possibly use of oral contraceptives. Having intercourse at an early age was dangerous because—as explained earlier—her immature cervix had a larger transformation zone, containing cells that are more susceptible to infection. These vulnerable cells form a bright red circle in the center of the cervix. Delia's teenage cervix provided a larger target area for infection than if she had waited until she was older.[8] With each new man in her life, Delia increased the likelihood of infection because men are not screened unless they have symptoms. As a result, there is a huge pool of infected men unknowingly passing the infection along, especially on college campuses.[9] If Delia is like the majority of college students, she's used condoms inconsistently.[10] Finally, there's the pill. It's suspected, but not yet proven, that oral contraceptives may facilitate infection by enlarging the transformation zone,[11] or by decreasing the amount of menstrual blood, which can act to flush the bacteria down and out.

But let's think positive. Let's assume Delia's treatment was effective, the antibiotics eliminated the chlamydia, and her subsequent liaisons did not re-expose her. Her tubes are healthy, the plumbing is in order. She's out of the woods, right?

Not necessarily.

There's one more thing to consider—Delia's memory of the infection. Not her cognitive memory, the recall of details like the boy's name and what it was like to find out. It was ten years ago, her freshman year. She was a bit wild for a time, did her share of drinking and partying: it was a phase. She hardly remembers the details—what for?

We're not talking names, places, when, and how. Delia carries in her a different sort of memory—an immunological one. And although she may have forgotten the chlamydia affair, her white cells surely have not.

It works like this. While the chlamydia were hiding out in Delia's cells, they made a type of protein called hsp. This molecule has many different jobs and comes in lots of varieties. The hsp was released when the cell died. Her white cells, on the patrol for alien matter, correctly identified the hsp as foreign, and made antibodies. In the process, the white cells memorized the architecture of the hsp.

Fast-forward a dozen years. An egg has been fertilized, and the embryo is newly implanted in Delia's uterus. A positive pregnancy test! She's overjoyed. But one of the first proteins the embryo makes is a type of hsp, and it's very similar to the chlamydial hsp. That's not good. White cells see the new hsp and can't tell the difference—they think it's the chlamydia infection acting up. They signal for help. Specialized fighter cells and toxins arrive, ready to destroy. They believe their target is a hostile invader, but it's not. It's the embryo.

This autoimmune mechanism causes early pregnancy loss and decreased in vitro fertilization success, even years after an apparently successful antibiotic treatment.[12] This was first published in the medical literature in 1994. Delia was in tenth grade, fifteen years old. By the time she entered college, were young women warned? Could she have known?

No, on both counts. And what's puzzling is that today's college students—unless they happen to subscribe to *Infectious Diseases in Obstetrics and Gynecology*—also can't possibly know.

This is alarming. Medical journals tell of finding chlamydial DNA in fallopian tubes, even after treatment, and describe how chlamydial hsp causes miscarriage years after silent infections.[13] They report that antibiotics might be more successful if extended to one week, instead of the current recommendation of one day.[14] But Delia doesn't read these journals. She gets her STD information from other sources, and those sources depict chlamydia as easy to detect and treat. For example, consider the Columbia University health information Web site goaskalice.com. Here Delia would learn that if she screens positive for the bacteria, she'll take a "simple and effective" course of antibiotics. In a few months, she'll return for retesting, but in the meantime, she can rest assured—only untreated infections cause sterility.

Let's take a closer look. First, consider the detection process. The question of who to screen, and how often, is open to question. The recommendation to screen women annually is arbitrary, based in part on cost-effectiveness.[15] The test is expensive, and the argument is made that the extra cases detected with more frequent screening do not justify the expenditure. Some experts propose more frequent screening for high-risk groups like women under twenty-five, maybe every six months.[16] Others have shown that treatment of asymptomatic men will reduce disease in women, but no one screens asymptomatic men.[17] Then there's the test itself. The gold standard these days is a urine test, but there is some risk of false negatives.[18] An infected woman who tests negative will believe she's fine, an assumption that could be perilous for herself and others. Next, the antibiotic "cure." Antibiotics cure chlamydia—sometimes. When they don't, the infection can persist for years, evading detection and damaging the tubes. Finally, years after an infection and regardless of treatment, an autoimmune reaction can occur, sometimes fatal to an embryo.

"Simple and effective" treatment for chlamydia? Not always. Not for everyone.

Student health and counseling centers are in a unique position to make these facts known to their students, and they know it. The editor of the *Journal of American College Health* put it this way: "Perhaps what most distinguishes college health from healthcare in any other form or setting is the opportunity it offers. . . . College health has the chance to marry a pivotal developmental moment with very focused resources to produce a greater probability that students will enjoy healthy lives."[19]

The opportunity is taken seriously, and health centers make it their responsibility to educate students about all sorts of health issues. To take an obvious example, they offer flyers on nutrition, explaining carbs, proteins, and saturated and unsaturated fat. Students learn that high cholesterol causes plaque, clogged arteries, and heart attacks. They know that sunscreen is necessary to protect against melanoma. And is anyone on campus unfamiliar with the finer points of exercise: aerobic, anaerobic, cardio, how often and for how long? The message is loud and clear: learn about good health, take care of yourself. There are consequences to your lifestyle, so work at changing it. Have the fruit instead of the pizza, take the stairs, not the elevator. Sure, it's not so fun, it takes discipline and self-control, but hey, that's what we've got to do to stay healthy. Later on, you'll be glad you did!

As another example, here's how the *Journal of American College Health* sees the issue of osteoporosis prevention:

> *College students of all ages deserve to be educated about the risk factors that lead to osteoporosis. Young women, in particular, need to be informed about how proper nutrition and regular exercise can help them achieve optimal peak bone mass. They need to be aware that a diet*

low in calcium and vitamin D as well as smoking, alco-
hol abuse, steroid use, high-protein diets, and both physi-
cal inactivity and excessive exercise may have a negative
impact on the lifetime health of their bone structure and
may predispose them to a higher risk of osteoporosis in
later years.[20]

Question: If there is a need to educate a twenty-something-year-old woman about the prevention of a postmenopausal condition, is there not an equal or greater need to make *sure* she's well informed about fertility?

Given that many college women postpone childbearing longer than ever, and others expose themselves to genital bacteria and viruses, one might wonder why we don't find a warning of *this* sort in the campus health literature:

College students of all ages deserve to be educated about
the risk factors that lead to infertility. Young women, in
particular, need to be informed about when is the opti-
mal period in their reproductive lives to conceive and de-
liver a healthy child. There are always exceptions, but
they need to be aware that often waiting until after age
thirty-five, as well as smoking, obesity, and having more
than one lifetime sexual partner, may have a negative
impact on their ability to conceive and may predispose
them to a higher risk of infertility, spontaneous abortion,
miscarriage, and childlessness in later years.

Questions for student health professionals: Where's the pamphlet on how to keep your reproductive system buffed? Where are women reminded that they have within them a sensitive ecosystem, where each month a complex, fine-tuned production takes place? How about introducing the terms *cervical transformation zone* and *chlamydial hsp* to the vocabulary of college women, so they can understand their physiology, and see clearly why promiscuity is so dangerous? Maybe there is a place in health promotion for some respect—even awe—for how a woman's body prepares for conception. And maybe there's a place for *this* warning: Don't take it for granted and mess with it, counting on a prescription to make it like new.

There's something else campus health centers can do. They can require all incoming students who are sexually active—both women and men—to be tested for chlamydia, the way international students are tested for tuberculosis. Just as healthy students deserve protection from a coughing, TB-infected classmate, young college women deserve protection from that popular frat boy, you know the one, who always has a few girls hoping to spend time with him over the weekend. He may be sharing more with them than his smile.

In the 1970s, a woman with tubal damage who could not conceive was sometimes told that maybe a virus had damaged her system in childhood. A doctor wanted to be able to tell his patient—distraught, hopeless, and desperate to understand what caused her condition—*something,* and having a reason helped her peace of mind.[21]

Now we are wiser. We know that for many women, the cause of their misery is this horrible little bug, and we know what it looks like, how it invades, and where it hides. But there's a gap between what we have discovered about chlamydia in the laboratory and what we communicate. What we know—and have known for over a decade—is sobering, but what we tell young people is sugarcoated. It's so over-simplified and incomplete as to border on misinformation.

How this happened and continues to happen, I don't know. But it is profoundly disconcerting that this is the case, when three million young women will be infected just this year. When I think of this information not reaching those who need it most, I see red. How dare anyone decide to withhold, not to fully inform? Who composes all the patient information, anyway, and who gives them the right to teach half-truths, to whitewash, sugarcoat, over-simplify, and reassure when there's still room for worry?

In how many of those women will chlamydia bring the nightmare of infertility or habitual miscarriage? With so much at risk, how can we fail to reach every young woman and spell it out: Even if you're "good," even if you get tested and take antibiotics, this bacteria can hurt you. *Sometimes there is no cure*. If you want to be a mother some-day, this bug can destroy your dream.

For women like Delia, having a family is one dream of many. When it comes to their dreams of grad school, travel abroad, a job, or financial stability, there's loads of guid-ance, all of it accurate and up-to-date: how to study for the SATs, get accepted to the right college, find a summer in-ternship, ace the GREs, get into grad school, complete a thesis, write a résumé, prepare for a job interview. But when it comes to their fertility, their knowledge is likely not so accurate. When it comes to that particular dream, they may not be so well informed. Is this another example of the PC agenda: sex without consequences, career over motherhood, women are just like men? It makes me livid to realize that, due to misinformation, whitewashing, and lack of warning, young women may be blind to the risks they are taking. How many of them will never know pregnancy and motherhood, experiences central to a woman's essence?

But it's too late to intervene; the harm's been done. Delia's on her way to Dallas, building her future, fully expecting to have it all: career, husband, kids. She's worked hard, and deserves to succeed. I hope fate will smile on her and grant her healthy, beautiful babies, as many as she wants. If not, she, like many others, will pay a heavy price.

CHAPTER VIII

Amanda's Thirty-ninth Birthday

Amanda Anderson, thirty-eight, is dreading her birthday. As it approaches, she sizes up her life—what she has, and what she hopes to have. She has: a master's in cell biology from Yale, a dozen publications, a devoted beagle, dear friends, and a career. She hopes to have: a husband and children.

Amanda always basked in her successes, and trusted that the rest would come in due time. Like many of her peers, she focused her time and energy on developing a career, and postponed the building of a family. In her early thirties she had a serious boyfriend, a fine man, who wanted to marry her. Amanda wasn't ready, so they broke up. Only her mother challenged the wisdom of that decision. Later, while celebrating the acceptance of her thesis, friends had joked that Mrs. Anderson would've preferred attending her daughter's bridal or baby shower. They enjoyed a good laugh.

Now it's not so funny. Amanda is in my office because as her birthday approaches, she is moody, irritable, and distracted. She is bored with her research and disenchanted

with university life. Amanda shares with me a new yearning, so profound it surprises her: to feel a new life inside her,
to give birth. My patient reports with astonishment that for
the first time, she envies friends—even strangers at the
market!—who are pregnant. She cries every day.

Amanda labored long and hard through school and
she'll get her Ph.D. nearly a decade after graduating from
college. There were setbacks due to changes in her thesis,
and conflict with advisers. There were also the years out of
school spent working in Europe and Africa. Grad school
has been endless, but finally her thesis is nearly finished,
and she's had offers from several universities for tenure-
track positions. But all that's not enough for Amanda now,
and she has begun to wonder . . . maybe Mom was right all
this time, that a woman's deepest fulfillment is in motherhood. Maybe Mom was right to bug her about marriage
and the passing of time. These and other troubling thoughts
distract my patient from her teaching and research, they
intrude while she is watching a movie or walking the dog,
and they keep her up at night. She is rethinking and doubt-
ing decisions made years ago about careers and boyfriends.
Most of the time, she feels certain she'll be able to have a
baby, because she's in excellent health, doesn't smoke, and
she's not "*that* old." Still, Amanda reports that last night
she had moments of panic: Could it be too late?

Amanda has reason to worry. Even if she soon falls in
love and marries (she has ruled out the single-mother option), her chances of conceiving each month have decreased
by 75 percent, compared to when she was thirty.[1] Of course,
it could still happen, if she's lucky. But if she does conceive,
the possibility of miscarriage has tripled, the rate of still-

birth has doubled, and the risk of genetic abnormality is six times as great.[2] Her pregnancy is more likely to be complicated by high blood pressure or diabetes, and her baby is more likely to be premature or low birth weight, conditions associated with neurological impairment as well as sudden infant death.

If Amanda cannot conceive naturally, and she and her husband want a biological child, her gynecologist will advise them to pursue assisted reproductive technology (ART). They will likely experience their first visit as difficult and stressful.[3] The couple will be examined and asked for details about their intimate life, with one another, and with others they may not care to recall. Following a series of tests, the analysis of semen and cervical mucus, and sometimes surgery, the cause of their infertility may or may not be found. Initial treatment is with fertility drugs, followed by in vitro fertilization (IVF). If Amanda is like many of the three million women who go through this process, she will face an awful ordeal.

How do women describe how they feel being unable to conceive, taking fertility drugs, or going through in vitro fertilization? What are the chances of success for Amanda, if she starts treatment at, say, age forty? And how much will it cost?

The answers are: angry, sad, helpless, guilty, bitter, resentful, and humiliated, "a state of desperation like nothing else,"[4] "an emotional roller-coaster," "PMS times a thousand," "the worst experience of my life"; 3 to 5 percent; and at least $20,000.

With women delaying childbearing as never before, the offices of fertility doctors are filled with fortysomething patients desperate for a baby. "Most of the women who come in here are healthy," said the director of the largest fertility clinic in San Francisco. "They're here because they're forty."[5] Amanda has a good chance of joining their ranks. Let's take a look at what may be ahead of her.

Clomid is the most popular fertility drug. It stimulates the ovaries, and encourages multiple eggs to mature. The time of ovulation is controlled and the chance of pregnancy maximized. Clomid commonly causes ovarian cysts, pelvic pain, hot flashes, nausea, breast tenderness, depression, and mood swings.[6] "Mood swings may be surprising and severe," warns the American Society of Reproductive Medicine's guide for patients.[7] There is an increased incidence of miscarriage and multiple births, and some studies show an increased risk of ovarian and breast cancer.[8] Clomid costs about $3,000 for one month's treatment, and most couples use it for four to six months. Amanda has a 5 to 10 percent chance per month of getting pregnant this way.

If Amanda needs IVF, she'd again take fertility drugs, and eggs would be removed surgically. They would be fertilized in the lab with her husband's sperm, and then transferred directly to her uterus. Each IVF attempt costs $15,000.

The emotional costs are high too. Women treated for infertility suffer from anxiety and depression as severely as do patients with cancer or cardiac disease.[9] After a failed IVF attempt, fears and anxiety intensify, memory and concentration worsen, and self-esteem falls. Patients perceive their infertility as a traumatic life event.[10] One forty-four-year-old woman whose only pregnancy ended in miscarriage a year earlier, and since then had spent thousands on hormones, said, "If you ever told me I'd be having this kind of difficulty, I would have laughed in your face. I exercise, I eat well, I keep better work hours, but I'm really not in control of what's happening with my little eggs. It's devastating. It's a terrible sense of failure."[11]

Of course, when treatment ends in success, parents will say it was all worth it. But success is rare. At age thirty-nine the chance of a live birth after an IVF attempt is 8 percent. By age forty-four, it falls to 3 percent.[12] This is why Dr. Zev Rosenwaks, medical director of infertility services at a major Manhattan medical center, warns, "If you are over forty, ART is unlikely to solve your infertility problem."[13]

If Amanda and her husband are willing to use a younger woman's egg, it will increase significantly the odds of having a baby. They may find this unacceptable however, because the child will have no genetic relationship with Amanda. This procedure costs $15,000 to $20,000.

That's the story. But educated as she is, Amanda is unlikely to be familiar with the risks of a first pregnancy in her forties, the ordeal of infertility, and the disappointing rate of success of ART. She may have some vague understanding that it is more difficult to get pregnant, that it doesn't happen as quickly. But she probably overestimates her chances of conceiving naturally and delivering a normal child at term, without complications or intervention.[14]

Many women share her misconceptions. A 2001 survey showed 89 percent of young, high-achieving women believed they would be able to get pregnant into their forties.[15] Another found that women have an excellent understanding of birth control, but they "overestimate the age at which fertility declines."[16] The former director of RESOLVE, a support network for couples coping with infertility, reports: "I can't tell you how many people we've had on our help line, crying and saying they had no idea how much fertility drops as you age."[17]

But how would they know? The media is constantly providing them with stories of babies born to older women, even grandmothers. For example, a woman like Amanda might take comfort in the recent headlines about a sixty-seven-year-old Romanian woman giving birth. Of course, she'd never wait *that* long, and yes, there are some ethical issues to consider, but the point she'd take from the news is that reproductive technology has given women control over their biology, and that at thirty-nine, she can safely wait to have children.

Should Amanda be reassured by the story of Adriana Iliescu, the oldest woman ever known to have given birth,[18] and by the well-publicized motherhood of celebrities like model Cheryl Tiegs (a mother at fifty-two), the late Pulitzer Prize–winning playwright Wendy Wasserstein (forty-eight), and actress Jane Seymour (forty-four)? The experts say no. They call the media coverage of these miracle births "the perpetuation of a dangerous myth." For example, Dr. Rosenwaks wrote in a *New York Times* editorial,

> *The nonstop media parade of midlife women producing offspring is stunning. . . . These stories are about the fortunate ones: they beat the odds. . . . As an infertility specialist, I often see women . . . who have been lulled into a mistaken belief that there is a medical technology that will allow women to have their genetic children when-*

ever they choose. . . . In our eagerness to outwit time, the media have made a bestseller out of the freshly minted fiction of "rewinding the biological clock."

We can't and we haven't.[19]

Dr. Rosenwaks was not alone in his effort to warn women. The largest professional organization of infertility doctors, the American Society of Reproductive Medicine (ASRM), sponsored a campaign in 2001 called Protect Your Fertility. Their ads highlighted the four major causes of infertility: advancing age, sexually transmitted diseases, smoking, and unhealthy weight. Like the media campaigns we've all seen discouraging cigarettes and drug use, the ads were placed on buses and in malls and theaters. But unlike the antitobacco and antidrug campaigns, the infertility ads were considered controversial and provocative. The ASRM drew the ire of the National Organization for Women (NOW), who argued that they sent a negative message to women who might want to delay or skip childbearing.[20] Mall and theater managers refused to make space available. The campaign died.

Thanks in part to these organizations, the message did not reach women like Amanda. A spokesman for ASRM pointed out the irony: "Our doctors were getting sick of hearing patients say, 'No one told me,' so we tried to educate women. Then we were accused by women's organizations of fear-mongering."[21]

One item Amanda probably *did* see is the publicity given a new company, Extend Fertility, and the service they provide—egg freezing. It would have been hard for her to miss the exposure. It was featured on NBC News

("Beating the Biological Clock"), *Good Morning America*, Fox News ("Egg Freezing May Offer Fertility Freedom"), *60 Minutes*, and *CBS Marketwatch*. There were articles in the *New York Times*, the *Washington Post*, *U.S. News and World Report* ("The Biological Clock on Ice"), *Nature* ("Age Is No Barrier"), *Newsweek*, *Forbes*, *Cosmopolitan*, and *Elle* ("Want to Hit the Snooze Button on your Biological Clock?").[22]

Egg freezing has been available since 1994 to women facing sterility due to chemotherapy. When Christy Jones, a thirty-four-year-old Harvard MBA, heard about it, she apparently saw dollar signs. Jones opened Extend Fertility, the first commercial facility to provide egg cryopreservation, in 2004. The business seeks to attract women like Amanda, who hope to outwit their biology.

One of the facility's press releases reads: "The days of the biological clock are over. In the past, women were bound by the limitations of time when it came to their reproductive choices. Women who wanted to get pregnant later in life were faced with egg quality issues. Now they have the option of extending their fertility by preserving their eggs at a time when they are much healthier. It's quite remarkable."[23] More recently they've moderated their claims, promising women "the opportunity to effectively slow down their biological clocks."[24]

But fertility specialists say the technology is not ready for marketing, that the company promotes unrealistic expectations, and that there is "a very high risk of exploitation of this patient population that is looking for hope. . . . Extend Fertility's Web site offers hope where many fertility experts would argue there is very little." The site claims success rates of 35 percent, called "unbelievable" by a world expert. The actual rate for successful birth using frozen eggs is closer to 2.5 percent.[25] Nonetheless, Extend Fertility is up and running in Los Angeles, New York, Boston, and Austin, Texas, ready to collect $10,000 for their services—financing is available—and another $400 a year for egg storage. And their Web site continues—evidently without any objections from NOW—to invite Amanda to "put her biological clock on ice."[26]

Maybe we shouldn't be surprised when NBC, CBS, and *Cosmopolitan*—or a CEO building her business—is less than responsible. They are permitted their agendas. So whose job is it, aside from Mrs. Anderson's, to remind Amanda of the possible consequences of waiting too long?

Well, to begin, how about the campus resources Amanda's been visiting for years for help in sorting out and planning her life? For instance, campus counseling and career centers state that their mission is to promote normal emotional development. Is parenthood an important part of adult development?

Erik Erikson thought so. This giant in the field of human development was the first to suggest that maturation is a lifelong process, from cradle to grave. Not only in childhood are there stages, each with certain tasks to be negotiated and mastered: to walk and talk, to be toilet-trained, and to make friends. Erikson's widely accepted theory holds that development continues into young and middle adulthood, and beyond. As in the growth of infants and toddlers, in adult development there is a built-in, biological thrust—a maturational push—to master the challenge at hand, and move on to the next. With each success, there is a change in the sense of self, there is growth and fulfillment.

According to Erikson, the tasks of young adulthood are intimacy, work, and generativity, the latter defined as "establishing and guiding the next generation." For most people, that means parenthood.[27]

Current studies confirm the importance of generativity. A Harvard researcher, who directed the longest prospective study of physical and mental health in the world, considers taking care of the next generation "a key to successful aging."[28] Another eminent authority in the field of child and adult psychiatry explains that responsible parenthood "propels development"[29] and leads to ongoing fulfillment on many levels—by the creation of a new person to love, by the opportunity to redefine one's relationship with parents and to appreciate and give back to them, by the maturation that is stimulated as relationships with children shift over time, and by turning to children and grandchildren in old age for solace, continuity, and hope.

Amanda wants these things. Her yearning for a child comes in part from the drive, the maturational pull, to take on a task central to this time in her life. It's hard-wired.

To avoid scenarios such as Amanda's, therefore, it seems logical for campus counselors to explore with a woman, in particular a woman nearing graduation, her thoughts and feelings about parenthood. This can be compared to the therapist bringing up issues of sexual identity, or autonomy from parents, with a client, and is consistent with the widely accepted view that counseling needs to recognize the "whole person."[30] If a woman indicates that motherhood is a goal, the therapist is in a position to educate her and to explain the risk of putting off childbearing indefinitely. Therapists, vocational counselors, career counselors—all these professionals have the opportunity to remind a young woman to give marriage and pregnancy some priority as she plans her career.

Sounds logical, right? Wrong. The psychologists writing in the American Psychological Association's guide *Career Counseling of College Students* have a different perspective.[31] In a chapter on counseling women, the authors focus on discrimination and "sociocultural indoctrination." For example, they cite problems of occupational and gender-role stereotypes, gender bias in education, the failure to encourage women to pursue careers, pay inequities, workplace harassment, the glass ceiling, and other "external barriers" as "pervasive and largely intractable."[32]

Career counselors, they write, are in an excellent position to intervene in issues relating to career and family. How? They can "highlight patterns of gender socialization that create imbalances in heterosexual two-job families."[33] They can offer workshops for the campus community that showcase working couples who successfully manage home and family. The authors suggest that gay and lesbian couples be included, as their perspectives "include highly creative, non-gender-stereotypic solutions to problems in managing the work-home interface." The only reference to children in this chapter, devoted specifically to guidance of women, is to say that their care can be a barrier to career success.

The authors urge counselors to "empower women to challenge patriarchal structures." They explain that "all professional activities are political acts,"[34] and argue that counselors who do not advocate for social change are implicitly maintaining an oppressive status quo, because their work does not attempt to challenge a society built on unequal access to power and privilege.[35]

Huh? Did I miss something? While it's true that there are still some instances of harassment or discrimination, for each patient with that complaint, I have fifty like Amanda: she's got the education/degree/career thing down, it's this love/marriage/family thing that she can't get right. The issues of on-site day care or managing home and family are problems she can only *dream* of having.

How about the student health center? Amanda drops by there a few times a year. Like most students, she buys the university-sponsored insurance plan every semester, and therefore the wellness center provides her medical care. Health-conscious and responsible, she comes in for treatment of minor ailments and for her annual women's health check. Since Amanda's arrival on campus at age thirty-two, she has dutifully appeared six times for this appointment. What happens at an annual woman's health check at the campus health center?

The visit begins with Amanda filling out a computerized questionnaire. Why are you here? Are you having any symptoms? Have you noticed a discharge, unusual odor, fever, irregular bleeding, or pain during intercourse? Are there any aspects of your sexual lifestyle which might have a bearing on your care? A new partner? A change in your sexual orientation? What type of contraception do you use? Have you had unprotected sex since your last menstrual period? Who do you have sex with—men, women, or both? Number of male lifetime partners? Number of female lifetime partners?

Amanda can then take a seat in the waiting room. On the counter is a cute basket shaped like a rabbit, filled with free condoms. She can pick up one of the health center's pamphlets: *What Every Woman Should Know about HIV/AIDS, Acquaintance and Date Rape, Contraception: Choosing a Method, Safer Sex, Woman to Woman: Three Steps to Health for Lesbian, Bisexual, or Any Women Who Have Sex with Women*.

Amanda then meets with a clinician, who examines her, performs a Pap smear, and screens for chlamydia, trichomonas, or gonorrhea infection. At the end of the appointment, there is time for "basic women's health education."

What topics are covered? At a minimum, women's health education is about performing monthly breast self-exams, getting regular exercise, and preventing osteoporosis. If needed, there is also discussion of contraceptives, drug or alcohol abuse, immunizations, and mental health issues like anxiety or depression. That's it.[36]

The average age of female students on campus is twenty-six.[37] Almost all plan to have children. They hear all the time about breast cancer and bone disease, the importance of exercise and a healthy diet. But from my review of campus health Web sites and pamphlets, I see no evidence that anyone is teaching these young women about the best time to have a family.

Not a surprise. The American College Health Association doesn't have it on their radar. A search of nearly all their journal archives turned up one 1983 article, "Fertility Awareness." Written by a nurse at the Berkeley Student Health Service, Fertility Awareness was a program on that campus instructing coeds how to examine their own mucus and cervix at various points in their cycle, in order to use "natural family planning."[38]

Yes, campus health centers make sure that Amanda has expertise at preventing pregnancy, but neglect to remind her of the biological limitations on childbearing. With this approach, they are following in the footsteps of many organizations claiming to advocate for women and their health.

"A powerful network of educated women" is how the American Association of University Women describes itself, and "reproductive rights" is one of the issues for which they advocate. "AAUW believes that individuals should be given complete and accurate information about their reproductive health and family planning options, ... only with reliable and complete information about their reproductive health can people make informed and appropriate decisions."[39] But a look at their list of position papers suggests that this group believes that the only challenges facing educated women is lack of access to sex education, birth control, and abortion. Here's their list of position papers:

- abstinence-only education (opposes)
- abortion coverage ban (opposes)
- emergency contraception (supports)
- attacks on reproductive choice "by extreme activist judicial nominees put forth by the Bush administration" (opposes)
- equity in contraception insurance coverage (supports)
- RU-486: nonsurgical abortion (supports)
- minor's access to "reproductive services without parental consent (supports)

- access to family planning regardless of income (supports)
- use of federal funds for abortions only when health of mother is at risk (opposes)

Is the AAUW unaware that the waiting rooms of infertility centers are crowded with professional women who bought the myth that they could wait, postpone, and wait some more until they decided it was the right time, only to end up with no choice at all about their reproduction? Should they not support educational campaigns like that of the ASRM, and have a position statement denouncing businesses targeting vulnerable women, urging them to invest in a controversial procedure? Why does only the distress of women with unwanted pregnancies reach the AAUW, and not the anguish of those mourning the pregnancies they will never have?

Like AAUW, Planned Parenthood's mission is to provide "accurate and complete information to make childbearing decisions," and to preserve "reproductive freedom—the fundamental right of every individual to decide freely and responsibly when and whether to have a child." Planned Parenthood advertises in campus newspapers, and is almost always found as a link on the Web sites of college health centers. What exactly would Amanda have learned from this organization if she had turned to them as a teen or young adult, and how would they have helped preserve her reproductive freedom?

Planned Parenthood describes three goals in their educational curriculum, which is designed to begin in pre-school. Their program seeks to: increase understanding of sexuality as a normal, healthy, lifelong aspect of human development; enhance awareness that there are differences in sexual expression and that sexuality is a personal matter; help individuals understand their sexuality, communicate their sexual feelings and decisions to others, and accept responsibility for their sexual decisions.[40]

In Planned Parenthood's *Young Woman's Guide to Sexuality*, Amanda would learn that "we are all sexual," and that "sexual expression is one of our basic human needs, like water, food and shelter." She'd read about sexual attraction, enjoying her body, and sexual relationships. She could take "The Perfect Partner Quiz": Does your partner carry condoms and help pay for other birth control? Does your partner have an annual checkup for sexually transmitted infections? Would your partner stand by you emotionally and financially if you got pregnant?

Nothing here, though, about those facts she learned in tenth grade but hasn't thought about since—that she was born with all the eggs she'll ever have, and that when she turns thirty, her eggs do too. One would assume that "reproductive choice" refers not only to the choice to prevent or terminate a pregnancy, but also to the choice to conceive and give birth. After all, isn't it *parenthood* that's supposedly being planned here? But on the topic of how a young woman can preserve her fertility and maximize her chances of becoming a mother, Planned Parenthood is silent.

Another organization reaching out to women like Amanda is the National Women's Health Network (NWHN). They declare themselves to be "a voice for women, a network for change." Their *Young Women's Health Packet*, 154 pages, is designed for girls ten to college age. In the Reproductive Health section, Amanda would find the usual instruction on STD identification and prevention, and get tips on broaching delicate subjects with a new partner, like sharing sexual histories and getting tested. She'd learn how using a condom can be fun. There's a first-person account here about having an abortion, and a list of states requiring parental consent to get one. And there are seven pages on the topic of masturbation.

From her appointments at the campus health, counseling, or career centers to the educational campaigns of AAUW, Planned Parenthood, and NWHN, it does not appear that preserving Amanda's fertility has much priority. In fact, it would appear to be a nonissue.

Of course, it's vital to provide Amanda with options for preventing pregnancy. But it is just as vital—especially given a mission of assuring "the right to reproductive freedom"— to offer her wisdom and clarity about when is the easiest and healthiest time to conceive.

In fact, there is such an obsession with *preventing* pregnancy, and with avoiding the bacteria and viruses that accompany promiscuity, there is such an inundation of information[41] about condoms, hormonal contraception, emergency contraception, abortion, the diaphragm, IUDs, HIV, HPV, Pap tests, chlamydia, gonorrhea, and warts, that a biological truth—one that Amanda sorely needed to hear— has been lost: pregnancy won't necessarily happen when *she* decides she's ready. There's a window of opportunity, then the window closes.

And with this lapse by the providers of "women's healthcare" begin many tales of heartache and despair.

Of course, some will argue it's too sensitive, it's too loaded an issue, patients will get upset. Ask a single woman who is carefully planning her career if she wants to have a family? Remind her the clock is ticking? No way! But we ask our patients difficult questions all the time. From bowel movements to suicide to genital warts—isn't that our job? We also feel obligated to warn patients about the consequences of their lifestyles, whether it be the dangers of cigarettes or junk food. When painful probing now may prevent worse suffering later, patients deal with it. A mammogram isn't fun, and a colonoscopy's no picnic, but we wouldn't dream of denying a patient these tests.

It's an apt comparison—infertility, miscarriages, and childlessness can be as awful as a lump in your breast.

Listen, if you're able, to excerpts from the story of one forty-five-year-old who survived three miscarriages:

> *I've wanted to be a mom all my life . . . I lean over and smile at infants in baby carriages and marvel at the sensations in my body. It's as though my flesh yearns to hold and hug a small body. . . . So I was deeply shocked by the idea I might be infertile. How could this be happening to me? . . . After four months on Clomid I got pregnant. We were ecstatic for eleven all-too-short weeks. Then I miscarried. . . . I will never forget the agony of seeing our partially formed baby outlined on the screen—stiff, still, and lifeless. That first loss was hard, very hard.*
>
> *A few months later we tried again. This time I did Clomid and something called HSG—a procedure that involves shooting stuff into your fallopian tubes to make sure that they are super clear. And sure enough I got pregnant. This time I miscarried in week thirteen. . . .*

*This second loss was even harder. . . . We were beginning
to believe we would have this baby. We had even picked
out some names.*

*After the second miscarriage we got deadly serious.
We took out a second mortgage on our house and signed
up for IVF. Twelve months and three cycles later I got
pregnant again, only to miscarry in week five. . . . I told
myself that this loss wasn't as bad as the others because it
was so early. Whether or not this was true, I knew I
needed to build some kind of wall between me and my
colossal, cumulative grief.*

*Those IVF cycles were completely debilitating—and
I'm not just talking about the money. For months we
were whiplashed by a treatment regime that jerked us
from hope to despair. The drugs and the procedures created huge stresses in my marriage and even undermined
the way I felt about my body. I began to resent my sexual
organs. I mean, if these parts and these functions turn
out to be completely useless, how can I do anything but
resent my big breasts and bloody periods. They are merely
burdensome."*[42]

I found this and other gut-wrenching interviews in the
book *Creating a Life: Professional Women and the Quest for
Children*. The author, Sylvia Ann Hewlett, set out to write
about the lives of highly educated, high-earning women as
they turned fifty. She intended to focus on the strategies
they used to break through the glass ceiling. After meeting
with ten women who were prominent in a diverse set of
fields, she confronted a remarkable fact: none of them had
children. And when she went back and explored further,

she learned that they all regretted their childlessness. It had not been a choice for any of them.

> *There is a secret out there, a painful, well-kept secret: At mid-life, between one third and one half of all high-achieving women in America do not have children. . . . The vast majority of these women did not choose to be childless. Looking back to their early twenties, when they graduated college, only 14 percent said they definitely had not wanted children.*
>
> *I had assumed that if these accomplished, powerful women were childless, surely they had chosen to be. I was absolutely prepared to understand that the exhilaration and challenge of a megawatt career made it easy to decide not to be a mother. Nothing could be further from the truth. When I talked to these women about children, their sense of loss was palpable. I could see it in their faces, hear it in their voices, and sense it in their words.*[43]

As a result of her unexpected finding, Hewlett decided to write instead about the struggle for children among successful career women. The interviews, grouped into chapters with titles like "Baby Hunger" and "The Sobering Facts," are a painful read. For example, there's this from the late Wendy Wasserstein:

> *For me, the reproductive thing has been huge . . . I have just spent seven years trying to have a child on my own. . . . By this point I've gone through so many procedures—and been injected with so many drugs—I can't even keep track of them all. What did I get out of all this? All I've*

proved is that I can't get pregnant, that I'm not really a girl. . . . I'm no longer sure that this new technology is remotely empowering. You take a woman of my generation, someone who is seriously accomplished, but is in her forties and hasn't had a child. This new technology becomes a way of telling her that whatever she accomplished, it isn't enough. And then when she fails to get pregnant—and most of us do fail—it erases her sense of professional competence and erases her confidence as a woman. I know these procedures left me feeling more depressed than at any other time in my life."*[44]

In addition, Hewlett writes, many of the high-achieving women who have children have fewer than they want, because they started too late. In her study, a majority of women with one child had wanted at least one more. "For many," she writes, "this is a source of deep regret." Let's listen to Sonia:

There are three of us who meet at a nearby health club Saturday mornings. Three women, each with one precious child. The pretense is exercise but we really meet to grieve. We sit in the juice bar and talk—and weep—and talk some more. . . . We share this aching loss around children we will never have. It sounds crazy, doesn't it? How can an imagined child provoke such deep grief? . . . Part of it is we all have much-loved older children and know what we are missing. . . . If only I had realized earlier on how fiercely I wanted that second child.[45]

---

* She conceived soon after this interview and had an emergency C-section in her sixth month; her daughter weighed under two pounds and spent ten weeks in the hospital.

"If only": these words capture the essence of this book. "If only women knew the facts; if only they were not blinded by hype and misinformation; if only they understood that if they wait they'll hit a wall."[46]

Remember, these are the women who got the high SAT scores and were valedictorians. They attended Harvard and Yale. They are surgeons, academics, CEOs. They've made it.

I have one question: *Shouldn't our daughters be warned?* For those women who include motherhood in their list of goals, shouldn't we do everything we can to prevent them from, as one childless professional put it, "inadvertently squandering [their] fertility"?[47] Of course, doing so would acknowledge the value of parenthood, and the differences between men and women. So don't hold your breath.

Here's a suggestion: As part of their basic women's health education, maybe student health centers should have, next to the condoms and date rape brochures, a few copies of Hewlett's book. Along with teaching breast self-exam and osteoporosis prevention, explain a woman's biology, that there is an optimal time for easy conception and birth. Tell women that just as there are advantages to delaying parenthood, so too there are risks, and suggest that they consider this information as they plan their careers.

They might also make available excerpts from a *Good Morning America* interview with Professor Adriana Iliescu, mentioned earlier, who had her first child at sixty-six using donor eggs. "I don't advise anyone to do what I did," she said. "My message is for young women to make an effort to have children in their youth. We should not count on miracles. Young women should learn from this that you can be-come desperate from not having a child."[48]

As for Amanda, her birthday came and went, and she survived. She's not yet counting on miracles, or desperate at not having a child. She's grateful for her friends, her dog, and the trips abroad. A fortysomething friend just be-came pregnant, so that was good news. Her mom stopped bugging her. Realistic or not, she manages to stay hopeful, most of the time. No doubt the Paxil helps too. She takes care of herself, tries to be upbeat, joined an online dating service, and avoids maternity stores. For now, it's one day at a time.

CONCLUSION

———

JOANNE IS A PSYCHOLOGIST COLLEAGUE OF MINE, AND I WANT to conclude by telling you about a conversation we had. We spoke about the omission at our center of questions about sexually transmitted diseases and abortions, and I shared my belief that this omission was unwise.

"Do *you* ask about them?" I asked, nervously.

"Of course I do! Every time. Otherwise I may be missing something big in the history."

"Well, *duh,*" we laughed together, in understood agreement. "Of course it's important to know if someone has herpes—it could be the whole reason behind their depression!"

We touched on some other charged subjects and found that we were in agreement on those, too: we'd always do what was best for our patients, but wouldn't necessarily publicize it. We then wondered how it could be that for years we worked side by side, yet this revealing exchange hadn't occurred earlier.

"Isn't it crazy," I said, "that we feel uncomfortable talking about these things?"

"Yes," she sighed. "But that's the way it is here. What can we do?"

Joanne sounded demoralized, and I gathered she was resigned to the situation. I know the feeling. But with the parade of Heathers, Staceys, and countless other calamities through my office, resignation is no longer an option. What can be done that I may stay true to my oath, "to prevent disease whenever I can," without worry of being discovered? What prevented Joanne and me from speaking years ago, and once we finally did, why did it feel like a confession, made in hushed tones, behind a closed door?

It was fear: we were afraid of challenging the entrenched dogma of our profession. The concerns Joanne and I shared about our patients—the physical and emotional harm of the anything-goes mentality, the devastating consequences of abortion, hookups, and STDs—are not politically correct. We feared sharing our views in an atmosphere perceived as intolerant; we were not prepared to risk malignment or ostracism.

What an outrage! Doesn't this preposterous situation in itself speak volumes about the alarming state of affairs we're in?

Like a patient unaware of his illness, the first step is acknowledgment that all is not well. We must recognize that campus counseling (in fact, all of mental health) as it now stands has been hijacked by repressive, radical ideologies. Open discussion is suppressed. Those who dissent are intimidated and silenced. Ideological diversity is nonexistent.

The next step is to realize that these radical agendas—promoted in the name of patient welfare and positive social change—are a prescription for disaster.

I fear that until we wake up, we will continue to puzzle over the campus epidemics of depression, eating disorders, cutting, and suicide. To be sure, the reasons for student distress are sometimes complex, but to the list of contributing factors we must add the campus culture of permissiveness, experimentation, androgeny, and spiritual bankruptcy. And we must see, as well, how this culture pervades our work.

That day seems far away. The authors of the recent Harvard book[1] about campus health, mentioned previously, see it differently. "This is a book about the extraordinary increase in serious mental illness on college campuses today and what we can do about it," the authors write. To their credit, they are right on target to acknowledge "gender differences" in relationships, and the negative consequences of promiscuity. They also mention the "tremendous emotional pain"[2] of unwanted pregnancy and abortion.

Great so far, but then they toe the line. Here we go again, with the same old mantras: students must get enough sleep and exercise, eat well ("substitute whole wheat bread for white bread, have a bowl of fortified cereal instead of a bagel or doughnut"), organize their time, stay in touch with family . . . Come on, Harvard expert, get real. You know a majority of students seeking our help are young women,[3] and that many tell stories like Heather and Olivia. You know that they are more susceptible to heartbreak and microbes, and when added to the stress of finals and sleep deprivation, it's often these that push them over the edge. Aren't your patients emptying tissue boxes like mine, miserable about their poor choices and abnormal Paps?

Forget the whole wheat bread. It's time we turn our

attention to deeper matters. So many young women at a critical stage of their development come to us in crisis and tell us their secrets. At my center, almost 70 percent of patients are women. They are vulnerable, and have much to lose. What we say, or don't say, will have far-reaching effects: the responsibility is awesome.

Instead of offering platitudes, tell the freshman or sophomore who has turned to you about oxytocin. Describe the hidden epidemic of STDs and the dangers of casual liaisons, even with latex. Suggest that she wait, and find the intimacy she *really* wants, the kind that's meaningful and lasting. Care for her according to *her* needs, without the false notions of a modern ideology; be a *real* feminist.

But then again, maybe you want to keep your job. Lawrence Summers, ex-president of Harvard, suggested that the minds of men and women may be different. That's how he became ex-president.

If we want to be successful in confronting the mental and physical health crisis of students, we need straight talk with all the sobering facts. We need a single agenda, and it has nothing to do with personal freedom or withholding judgment. It would start with expressing our belief in the tremendous potential of youth, and a vote of confidence in their ability to make wise decisions. The message would be: you are responsible for yourselves and you will determine your futures. The decisions you make each day make a difference. One way we differ from animals is having our *heads* above our *hearts;* the brain can control the heart and its urges. Sure, it's difficult; sure, it's an ideal; but we want you to strive for it. You can do this; you can change. We have faith in you.

That's a message that elevates and inspires young people, and that's the sort of message we lack on our campuses. Instead, we offer "Sex-Tac-Toe,"[4] condom races,[5] and students in banana costumes[6] handing out free birth control. Is this the best we can do? If we are juvenile, why should they behave like grown-ups?

We should expect more from our patients, but at the same time, we must recognize their vulnerability and the opportunity to make a difference.

For example, say a twenty-four-year-old woman comes in for her annual exam. In addition to a discussion of diet, exercise, and sexual orientation, she should be asked if motherhood is on her list of life goals. If it is, she needs to understand some basic statistics.[7] She should be cautioned about media attention paid to women having their first child in their forties—often those mothers have no genetic relationship with their babies, and their fertilization procedures may have cost more than their student loans. She should learn that fertility declines at thirty, and be warned that she could be exploited by businesses such as egg freezing. It won't hurt for her to keep this information in the back of her mind as she makes decisions about relationships and career.

Inform young people about HIV without distortion, and to those with risky behaviors, convey the moral obligation to be tested. Provide explicit information that may be disturbing. Nature exists; if you don't like what biology suggests about your ideology, maybe it's time to take another look at your ideology.

STDs: Sound an alarm that's explicit and matter-of-fact. Allow me to say to the Brians and Heathers in my practice: Your behaviors are hazardous; you are jeopardizing your health. Here's *why* and here's *how* to avoid them. Doctor's orders! Vaccines are great, but relying on biotechnology to protect us from risky behaviors is foolish.

Campus mental health must wake up to the reality that many students who come to us have an STD. It could be warts, herpes, or "just" an abnormal Pap—don't underestimate how devastating these may be. Mind you: like sexual abuse in childhood, having an STD may be a secret that students won't share unless we ask.[8] It's essential, therefore to include questions about STDs in our intakes, and keep these epidemics in mind as we consider students' depression, worrying, and poor self-esteem.

Include evidence that sometimes screening tests aren't accurate, and antibiotics may not always cure. And in designing the pamphlets meant to warn, please omit the suggestive photos.[9] There's no romance in bacterial infection. Think instead of the anti-tobacco ads—the Marlboro Man saying, "Bob, I've got emphysema."

There's nothing wrong with fear, if it is based in reality; we use it all the time in health. Here's a list (partial, I'm sure) of things we're told to fear: secondhand smoke, MSG, extra pounds, pesticides, saturated fats, Ritalin and Adderall, seesaws, dodge ball, sitting in the sun. And how about the "anybody can get AIDS" myth, and the needless anxiety that results? I don't hear anyone complaining about "fear tactics" there.

Acknowledge gender differences. If you doubt these exist, pick up a recent textbook on the subject edited by a Columbia University expert—it covers everything from humor to gallbladders. ". . . women differ from men in significant ways in every system of the body," the author writes. "It's a little like the California gold rush: Everywhere you look, a new fact, unique to one of the sexes, is apparent."[10] Be careful: the book weighs ten pounds. Or you may want to take a look at *As Nature Made Him: The Boy Who Was Raised as a Girl*[11]—required reading for anyone who believes the hoax that nurture is stronger than nature. The blurring of differences between male and female is a radical agenda unsupported by hard science.

To our colleges and universities: stop the normalization of behaviors that many therapists—not to mention parents of your students—consider depraved. Again, that this even needs to be said is indicative of the sad state we're in.

Admit the trauma, to some women and some men, of abortion. Reach out to those for whom the experience has *not* been an opportunity for "growth and maturation."[12] Provide a support group; at the very least ask about it!

The exaggerated place of sexuality is grotesque[13] and destructive. *We are not defined by our urges*—straight, gay, lesbian, or bi. What sort of message is that to our youth? We are defined by something more essential, uplifting, and transcendent. I fear this ideology that enshrines the body (health, appearance, physical pleasure) and abandons the soul (meaning, self-sacrifice, family, church).

Recognize that for many students, faith may be a tool to promote mental health. In sorting out the dilemma of suicides on campus, consider if perhaps the soullessness and angst of secularism contributes. When patients struggle with suicide, discussion of ultimate issues like meaning, purpose, and God are imperative. Acknowledge the benefits of self-restraint in areas other than diet, tobacco, and alcohol. Self-discipline exists outside the cafeteria and the gym.

And one last thing: don't tell me how to speak and what to think—I do that just fine, thank you.

You probably want to know how all these stories end. I'll tell you what I know: Heather realized her "friend with benefits" had nothing to do with friendship or benefits. Stacey has a type of HPV that can cause cancer; she'll need a Pap every six months for the next two years. Brian reassured me he'd be careful, but, as far as I know, he never went for testing. Amanda is forty-one and no closer to motherhood than she was at thirty-eight. Ned paid for private therapy, because there wasn't anyone on our staff who shared his values. Sarah was thrilled to have her sixth child, and never went to law school. Sophia is HIV negative, and is getting a divorce. Kelly was placed on medication, but never came back to see me.

In 1997 I went to the annual meeting of the American Academy of Child and Adolescent Psychiatry. The Belgian film *Ma Vie en Rose* was shown and discussed. It told the story of a boy distressed by his boyness, who yearned only for female things: pink toile dresses, earrings, lipstick. Ludovic insisted that he is a girl, that he would grow breasts and menstruate, and someday be someone's bride. As a result, he and his family suffered humiliation and disdain; his father lost his job. It was a superb film and it evoked compassion for the boy and his family.

The discussion that followed focused on Ludovic's victimization in a society with rigid definitions of male and female. If his culture did not insist on a black-and-white understanding of sexuality, my colleagues argued, he would have had an easier time. The implication was that society must change.

I raised my hand to say that it was the boy who was disordered, not society. I looked around and listened. It dawned on me that my comment would not be well received. I didn't have the guts to be the sole challenger, and I lowered my hand.

Nine years later, my hand is up again.

NOTES

INTRODUCTION

1. Robert Gallagher, *National Survey of Counseling Directors* (Alexandria, Va.: International Association of Counseling Services, 2005).

2. A. Levine and J. Cureton, "What We Know about Today's College Students," *About Campus*, March–April 1998.

3. Domeena C. Renshaw, "Sex and the 1980s College Student," *Journal of American College Health* 37, no. 4 (1989): 156.

4. Bert Meisenbach, "Is Value-Free Sex Talk Valuable?," *Journal of American College Health* 40, no. 2 (1991): 99.

5. John F. Lewis, Robert M. Malow, and Susan J. Ireland, "HIV/AIDS Risk in Heterosexual College Students: A Review of a Decade of Literature," *Journal of American College Health* 45, no. 4 (1997): 153.

6. www.stuorg.iastate.edu/cuffs/; www.ac.wwu.edu/~sweete/; www.columbia.edu/cu/cv.

7. American Psychological Association, Committee on Lesbian and Gay Concerns, "Avoiding Heterosexual

Bias in Language," *American Psychologist* 46, no. 9 (Sept. 1991): 973–74; www.apastyle.org/sexuality.html.

8. www.hedir.org/2004award.htm.

9. For example, when the editor of *Psychology Today* ran a small ad in the back of the magazine for Joseph Nicolosi's book *A Parent's Guide to Preventing Homosexuality*, he received threats and insults: Robert Epstein, "Am I Anti-Gay? You Be the Judge," *Psychology Today*, January–February 2003.

10. Rogers H. Wright and Nicholas A. Cummings, *Destructive Trends in Mental Health: The Well-Intentioned Path to Harm* (New York: Routledge, 2005); former president of the APA Robert Perloff speaking at the annual NARTH conference, Washington, D.C., November 2004; Dr. Nicholas Cummings, cited in Linda Nicolosi, "Psychology Losing Scientific Credibility, Say APA Insiders," www.narth.org, November 15, 2005.

11. U.S. Department of Education, Office of Educational Research and Improvement, *Digest of Education Statistics* (Washington, D.C.: U.S. Department of Education, Office of Educational Research and Improvement, 2004).

CHAPTER 1. UNPROTECTED

1. Robert E. Rector, Kirk A. Johnson, and Lauren R. Noyes, "Sexually Active Teenagers Are More Likely to Be Depressed and to Attempt Suicide," Heritage Center for Data Analysis, 2003, www.heritage.org.

2. K. Joyner and R. Udry, "You Don't Bring Me Any-

thing but Down: Adolescent Romance and Depression," *Journal of Health and Social Behavior* 41, no. 4 (December 2000): 369–91.

3. See also Deeanna Franklin, "Romantic Stress Tied to Depression in Sensitive Girls," *Clinical Psychiatric News*, April 2005, 31; and Denise D. Hallfors et al., "Which Comes First in Adolescence—Sex and Drugs or Depression?" *American Journal of Preventive Medicine* 29, no. 3 (2005): 163–70.

4. American College Health Association, *Position Statement on Tobacco on College and University Campuses* (Baltimore: American College Health Association, 2000).

5. This is a complex subject. Men also release oxytocin and vasopressin, causing attachment, but testosterone has the opposite effect. I focus on women because in my practice they are more often confused and distressed about casual sexual relationships than men.

6. K. Christensson et al., "Effect of Nipple Stimulation on Uterine Activity and on Plasma Levels of Oxytocin in Full Term, Healthy, Pregnant Women," *Acta Obstetricia et Gynecologica Scandinavia* 68 (1989): 205–10; Larry J. Young and Zuoxin Wang, "The Neurobiology of Pair Bonding," *Nature Neuroscience* 7, no. 10 (Oct. 2004): 1048–54; K. M. Kendrick, "Oxytocin, Motherhood and Bonding," *Experimental Physiology* 85 (March 2000): 111S–124S.

7. Professor Diane Witt of State University of New York at Binghamton, cited in Susan E. Barker, "Re-

search Links Oxytocin and Socio-sexual Behaviors," www.oxytocin.org.

8. Ibid.

9. Michael Kosfeld, et al., "Oxytocin Increases Trust in Humans," *Nature* 435 (June 2005): 673.

10. A. R. Damasio, *Descartes' Error: Emotion, Reason, and the Human Brain* (New York: Penguin, 1994).

11. Richard E. Redding, "Sociopolitical Diversity in Psychology," *American Psychologist* 56, no. 3 (2001): 205–15.

12. Beth Azar, "When Research Is Swept under the Rug," *APA Monitor* 28, no. 8 (August 1997): 1.

13. Diane F. Halpern, Richard Gilbert, and Stanley Coren, "PC or Not PC? Contemporary Challenges to Unpopular Research Findings," *Journal of Social Distress and the Homeless* 5, no. 2 (1996): 251–70.

14. Redding, "Sociopolitical Diversity in Psychology"; Halpern et al., ibid.; Robert J. Sternberg, "Costs and Benefits of Defying the Crowd in Science," *Intelligence* 26, no. 3 (1998): 209–15.

15. www.goaskalice.com.

16. www.students.vcu.edu/counsel/safezone/trans_flyer _ncod.html.

17. http://campus.umr.edu/counsel/selfhelp/vpl/sexual choices.html.

18. www.uwec.edu/counsel/pubs/lgbtqrelationships.htm.

19. A phrase borrowed from literature from the Medical Institute for Sexual Health.

CHAPTER II. DAMAGE CONTROL

1. Read personal accounts of treatment at hpvsupport. com, health.groups.yahoo.com, and many other sites.

2. Sebastian Faro, *Sexually Transmitted Diseases in Women* (Baltimore: Lippincott, Williams and Wilkins, 2003), 163; Cynthia A. Taylor, Mary L. Keller, and Judith J. Egan, "Advice from Affected Persons about Living with Human Papillomavirus Infection," *Journal of Nursing Scholarship* 29, no. 1 (1997): 27–32.

3. Faro, *Sexually Transmitted Diseases*, 167.

4. Joel Palefsky, *What Your Doctor May Not Tell You About HPV and Abnormal Pap Smears* (New York: Warner Books, 2002), 39.

5. National Institute of Allergy and Infectious Disease, NIH, "Workshop Summary: Scientific Evidence on Condom Effectiveness for STD Prevention, 2001," http://www.niaid.nih.gov/dmid/stds/condomreport.pdf.

6. Gloria Ho et al., "Natural History of Cervicovaginal Papillomavirus Infection in Young Women," *New England Journal of Medicine* 338, no. 7 (1998): 423–28.

7. American College Health Association, *Making Sex Safer* (Baltimore: American College Health Association, 2002).

8. L. J. Burak and M. Meyer, "Factors Influencing College Women's Gynecological Screening Behaviors and Intentions," *Journal of Health Education* 29, no. 6 (1998): 365–70, cited in Kimberly Ingledue, Randall Cottrell, and Amy Bernard, "College Women's Knowledge, Perceptions, and Preventive Behaviors

Regarding Human Papillomavirus Infection and Cervical Cancer," *American Journal of Health Studies* 19, no. 1 (2004): 28; Thomas C. Wright and Mark Schiffman, "Adding a Test for Human Papillomavirus DNA to Cervical-Cancer Screening," *New England Journal of Medicine* 348, no. 6 (2003): 489–90; Palefsky, *What Your Doctor May Not Tell You*, 47.

9. Palefsky, *What Your Doctor May Not Tell You*, 44.

10. S. Edwards, "Human Papillomavirus Infection Is Associated with Multiple Partners," *Family Planning Perspectives* 26, no. 3 (1994); Lisa A. Manhart and Laura Koutsky, "Do Condoms Prevent Genital HPV Infection, External Genital Warts, or Cervical Neoplasia?" *Sexually Transmitted Diseases* 29, no. 11 (2002): 725–35; R. L. Winer et al., "Genital Human Papillomavirus Infection: Incidence and Risk Factors in a Cohort of Female University Students," *American Journal of Epidemiology* 157, no. 3 (2003): 218–26; National Institute of Allergy and Infectious Diseases, "Scientific Evidence on Condom Effectiveness for STD Prevention," workshop summary, June 12–13, 2000. From the testimony of Tom Coburn, M.D., before the U.S. House of Representatives Subcommittee on Criminal Justice, Drug Policy and Human Resources, hearing on Cervical Cancer and Human Papillomavirus, March 11, 2004: "In a February 19, 1999 letter . . . Dr. Richard D. Klausner, then-director of the National Cancer Institute, stated, 'condoms are ineffective against HPV.' " The science in this regard is so clear that Dr. Klaus-

ner concluded, "additional research efforts by NCI on the effectiveness of condoms in preventing HPV transmission are not warranted" (http://www.house. gov/reform).

11. The same is true for herpes.

12. Constance Mao et al., "Clinical Findings among Young Women with Genital Human Papillomavirus Infection," *American Journal of Obstetrics and Gynecology* 188 (2003): 677–84.

13. John E. Lewis, Robert M. Malow, and Susan J. Ireland, "HIV/AIDS Risk in Heterosexual College Students," *Journal of American College Health* 45, no. 4 (1997): 147–67; Bruce Jancin, "Despite Guidelines, U.S. Condom Use Still Low," *Clinical Psychiatry News*, January 2004, 66; Kathy A. Douglas et al., "Results from the 1995 National College Health Risk Behavior Survey," *Journal of American College Health* 46, no. 2 (1997): 55–66; National College Health Assessment Spring 2003 Reference Group Report, *Journal of American College Health* 53, no. 5 (March/April 2005): 205.

14. For anal intercourse condom use was 23 percent.

15. Renee M. Oncale and Bruce M. King, "Comparisons of Men's and Women's Attempts to Dissuade Sexual Partners from the Couple Using Condoms," *Archives of Sexual Behavior* 30, no. 4 (2001): 379.

16. Richard Crosby et al., "Condom Use Errors and Problems among College Men," *Sexually Transmitted Diseases* 29, no. 9 (2002): 552–57.

17. Palefsky, *What Your Doctor May Not Tell You*, 82;

"Sensitivity of PAP for identifying women with cervical cancer or its precursor condition ranges from 51% to 85%," www.womeningovernment.org/prevention/hpv_cervicalcancer_info.asp.

18. www.papsmearsuitagainstmagee.com/media.htm. As of this writing, the class action suit was dismissed, but is being appealed. Individual lawsuits are proceeding.

19. Jerome Groopman, "Contagion: A sometimes lethal epidemic that condoms can't stop," *New Yorker*, September 13, 1999, 34. See also the case cited in the testimony of Tom Colburn, M.D., to the House Subcommittee as cited in note 10.

20. American College Health Association, "HPV ... What's *That?*" 2003, www.ashastd.org.

21. Palefsky, *What Your Doctor May Not Tell You*, 38–39.

22. One authority, David Hager, M.D., communicated to me (3/17/06) that HPV may persist in 10 percent to 12 percent of women.

23. Victor Moreno et al., "Effect of Oral Contraceptives on Risk of Cervical Cancer in Women with Human Papillomavirus Infection: The IARC Multicentric Case-Control Study," *Lancet* 359 (2002): 1085.

24. Palefsky, *What Your Doctor May Not Tell You*, 19.

25. Faro, *Sexually Transmitted Diseases*.

26. Celine A. Hamilton and Gail Bauchman, "Health Education for Adolescents with Abnormal Pap Smears," *Journal of the American Medical Women's Association* 54 (1999): 149–51.

27. American College Health Association, "HPV ... What's *That?*": "Now I realize everyone who has sexual contact is at risk."

28. American Social Health Association, www.ashastd. org.

29. Hunter Handsfield, M.D., on www.hpvsupport.com.

30. J. W. Richards and A. Blum, "Health Promotion," in *Family Medicine Principles and Practice*, 3rd ed., ed. R. B. Taylor (New York: Springer-Verlag, 1986), 101, cited in Roselyn Payne Epps and Marc W. Manley, "A Physician's Guide to Preventing Tobacco Use during Childhood and Adolescence," *Pediatrics* 88, no. 1 (1991): 140–44.

31. Lorena M. Siqueira, M.D., as quoted in Damian McNamara, "Straight Talk Can Head Off Teen Binge Drinking," *Clinical Psychiatry News*, April 2005, 34.

32. Kathryn Jean Lopez, "Looking for Love in All the Wrong Ways," nationalreview.com/nr_comment/nr_ commentprint7300la.html (2001); see also Daniel McGinn, "Mating Behavior 101" on msnbc.msn.com/ id/6100311/site/newsweek/ (2004); Elizabeth L. Paul, Brian McManus, Allison Hayes, " 'Hookups': Characteristics and Correlates of College Students' Spontaneous and Anonymous Sexual Experiences," *The Journal of Sex Research* 37, no. 1 (February 2000): 76.

33. Perhaps individual practitioners do this, but I see no priority given this subject on campus health education Web sites, or in their support groups, workshops, conferences, and journals—aside from the suggestion to "limit partners."

34. Medical Institute for Sexual Health, *You Have Been Given an Incredible Gift*. Power Cord Communications, P.O. Box 24246, Waco, TX 76702-4246.

35. Marcia Shew et al., "Interval between Menarche and

First Sexual Intercourse, Related to Risk of Human Papillomavirus Infection," *Journal of Pediatrics* 125 (1993): 665; Anna-Barbara Moscicki et al., "Differences in Biologic Maturation, Sexual Behavior, and Sexually Transmitted Disease between Adolescents with and without Cervical Intraepithelial Neoplasia," *Journal of Pediatrics* 115 (1989): 488; Palefsky, *What Your Doctor May Not Tell You*, 19.

36. American College Health Association, "HPV ... What's *That*?"

37. American College Health Association, *Sexually Transmitted Diseases: What Everyone Should Know* (Baltimore: American College Health Association, 2003).

38. "Cervical Cancer and Human Papillomavirus": Hearing before the Subcommittee on Criminal Justice, Drug Policy and Human Resources of the Committee on Government Reform, U.S. House of Representatives, March 11, 2004.

39. *Webster's Universal College Dictionary* (New York: Random House, 1997).

CHAPTER III. MEMO TO THE APA:
BELIEVING IN GOD IS GOOD FOR YOU

1. Edward P. Shafranske and H. Newton Maloney, "Clinical Psychologists' Religious and Spiritual Orientations and Their Practice of Psychotherapy," *Psychotherapy* 27, no. 1 (Spring 1990): 72–78.

2. Ibid.; Allen E. Bergin and Jay P. Jensen, "Religiosity of Psychotherapists: A National Survey," *Psychotherapy* 27, no. 1 (Spring 1990): 3–7.

3. Shafranske and Maloney, "Clinical Psychologists' Religious and Spiritual Orientations."

4. E. Shafranske, "Religiosity of Clinical and Counseling Psychologists," unpublished manuscript, 1995, cited in Edward P. Shafranske, *Religion and the Clinical Practice of Psychology* (Washington, D.C.: American Psychological Association, 1996), 154.

5. Ibid., 152.

6. Bergin and Jensen, "Religiosity of Psychotherapists."

7. J. Gartner et al., "The Effect of Client and Counselor Values on Clinical Judgement," *Counseling and Values* 35 (October 1990).

8. UCLA Higher Education Research Institute, "Spirituality in Higher Education: A National Study of College Student's Search for Meaning and Purpose," www.sprituality.ucla.edu.

9. As opposed to "spiritual" students, who believe "we are all spiritual beings," and believe in "the sacredness of life." Spirituality had a mixed relationship with psychological health, but religious involvement had a clearly positive association.

10. American College Health Association Board of Directors, *Cultural Competency Statement*, July 2000.

11. William T. O'Donohue, "Cultural Sensitivity: A Critical Examination," in *Destructive Trends in Mental Health: The Well-Intentioned Path to Harm*, ed. Rogers H. Wright and Nicholas A. Cummings (New York: Routledge, 2005), 29–44.

12. It is inaccurate to imply that college health and counseling avoids discussion of all religious cultures. At the 2005 meeting of the American College Health

Association, a session called "Providing Culturally Appropriate Health Care to Diverse Populations: A Focus on Muslim Women" was presented.

13. I later learned that almost 14 percent of the student population identify themselves as born-again Christian, and almost 20 percent as Roman Catholic.

14. American Psychiatric Association, *Practice Guidelines for the Treatment of Psychiatric Disorders* (Arlington, Va.: American Psychiatric Association 2004), 877; Harold G. Koenig, *Handbook of Religion and Mental Health* (San Diego, Calif.: Academic Press, 1998), 169–70; Leilani Greening and Laura Stoppelbein, "Religiosity, Attributional Style, and Social Support as Psychosocial Buffers for African American and White Adolescents' Perceived Risk for Suicide," *Suicide and Life-Threatening Behavior* 32, no. 4 (2002): 404–17.

15. Kevin M. Malone et al., "Protective Factors against Suicidal Acts in Major Depression," *American Journal of Psychiatry* 157 (2000): 1084–88.

16. Sometimes religious involvement can have harmful effects, but mostly there is a positive association with better health. See Jeffrey S. Levin and Linda M. Chatters, *Research on Religion and Mental Health: An Overview of Empirical Findings and Theoretical Issues*, in *Handbook of Religion and Mental Health*, ed. Harold G. Koenig (San Diego, Calif.: Academic Press, 1998), 33–50.

17. I. Orbach et al., "Mental Pain and Its Relationship to Suicidality and Life Meaning," *Suicide and Life-Threatening Behavior* 33, no. 3 (2003): 231–41.

18. Andrew P. Tix and Patricia A. Frazier, "The Use of Religious Coping during Stressful Life Events: Main Effects, Moderation, and Mediation," *Journal of Consulting and Clinical Psychology* 66, no. 2 (1998): 411–22; K. O. Eli et al., "Social Support, Sense of Control, and Coping among Patients with Breast, Lung, or Colorectal Cancer," *Journal of Psychosocial Oncology* 7 (1989): 63–88; K. I. Pargament, B. W. Smith, and H. G. Koenig, *Religious Coping with the Oklahoma City Bombing: The Brief RCOPE*, paper presented at the 104th Annual Convention of the American Psychological Association, Toronto, August 1996; C. L. Park and L. H. Cohen, "Religious and Nonreligious Coping with the Death of a Friend," *Cognitive Therapy and Research* 17 (1993): 561–77; and D. N. McIntosh, R. C. Silver, and C. B. Wortman, "Religion's Role in Adjustment to a Negative Life Event: Coping with the Loss of a Child," *Journal of Personality and Social Psychology* 65 (1993): 812–21.

19. Lisa Miller and Merav Gur, "Religiosity, Depression, and Physical Maturation in Adolescent Girls," *Journal of the American Academy of Child and Adolescent Psychiatry* 41, no. 2 (2002): 206–14.

20. Michael J. Donahue and Peter L. Benson, "Religion and the Well-Being of Adolescents," *Journal of Social Issues* 51, no. 2 (1995): 145–60.

21. E. James Anthony and Bertram J. Cohler, *The Invulnerable Child* (New York: Guilford Press, 1987), 38.

22. Gail Ironson and George Solomon, "The Ironson-Woods Spirituality / Religiousness Index Is Associated

with Long Survival, Health Behaviors, Less Distress, and Low Cortisol in People with HIV/AIDS," *Annals of Behavioral Medicine* 24, no. 1 (2002): 34–48.

23. H. G. Koenig et al., "The Relationship between Religious Activities and Blood Pressure in Older Adults," *International Journal of Psychiatry in Medicine* 28 (1998): 189–213.

24. Daniel E. Hall, "Religious Attendance: More Cost-Effective than Lipitor?" *Journal of the American Board of Family Medicine* 19 (2006): 103–9.

25. Lynda Powell, M.D., cited in Kevin Helliker, "Body and Spirit: Why Attending Religious Services May Benefit Health," *Wall Street Journal*, May 3, 2005.

26. Robert A. Hummer et al., "Religious Involvement and U.S. Adult Mortality," *Demography* 36, no. 2 (1999): 273–85; Lynda H. Powell, Leila Shahabi, and Carl E. Thoresen, "Religion and Spirituality: Linkages to Physical Health," *American Psychologist* 58, no. 1 (2003): 36–52.

27. Joanna Maselko, "Forgiveness Is Associated with Psychological Health: Findings from the General Social Survey," www.forgiving.org/conference_archive/conference2.asp; Robert A. Emmons and Michael E. McCullough, "Counting Blessings versus Burdens: An Experimental Investigation of Gratitude and Subjective Well-Being in Daily Life," *Journal of Personality and Social Psychology* 84, no. 2 (2003): 377–89; and Suzanne C. Segerstrom et al., "Optimism Is Associated with Mood, Coping, and Immune Change in Response to Stress," *Journal of Personality and Social Psychology* 74, no. 6 (1998):

1646–55. Eric Giltay (2004) Dispositional Optimism all All-Cause and Cardiovascular Mortality in a Prospective Cohort of Elderly Dutch Men and Women, *Archives of General Psychiatry* 61, 1126–35.

28. Levin and Chatters, *Research on Religion and Mental Health*, 34–35.

29. D. B. Larson, J. P. Swyers, and M. E. McCullough, eds., *Scientific Research on Spirituality and Health: A Consensus Report* (Rockville, Md.: National Institute for Healthcare Research, 1998); and G. H. Gallup, *Religion in America* (Princeton, N.J.: Gallup Organization, 1990).

30. D. A. Abbott, M. Berry, and W. H. Meredith, "Religious Belief and Practice: A Potential Asset in Helping Families," *Family Relations* 39 (1990): 443–48.

31. American Psychiatric Association, *Practice Guidelines*, 877; and Kanita Dervic et al., "Religious Affiliation and Suicide Attempt," *American Journal of Psychiatry* 161 (2004): 2302–8.

32. David H. Barlow and V. Mark Durand, *Abnormal Psychology: An Integrative Approach* (Belmont, Calif.: Thompson/Wadsworth, 2005); Eugene H. Rubin and Charles Zorumski, eds. *Adult Psychiatry*, 2nd edition (Malden, Mass.: Blackwell Publishing, 2005); Theodore A. Stern, John B. Herman, and Peter L. Slavin, eds., *Massachusetts General Hospital Guide to Primary Care Psychiatry*, 2nd edition (New York: McGraw Hill, 2004); Edwin S. Shneidman, *Comprehending Suicide: Landmarks in 20th Century Suicidology* (Washington, D.C.: American Psychological Association, 2001); Douglas A. Jacobs, ed., *Harvard Medical School*

Guide to Suicide Assessment and Intervention (San Francisco, Calif.: Jossey-Bass, 1999), Bruce Bongar, *The Suicidal Patient: Clinical and Legal Standards of Care*, 2nd ed. (Washington, D.C.: American Psychological Association, 2002); John A. Chiles and Kirk D. Strosahl, *The Suicidal Patient: Principals of Assessment, Treatment, and Case Management* (Arlington, Va.: American Psychiatric Press, 1995).

33. E. Lehr and B. Spilka, "A Systematic Review of Religion Found in Introductory Psychology Textbooks: A Comparison of Three Decades," *Journal for the Scientific Study of Religion* 28 (1989): 366–71; David H. Barlow and V. Mark Durand, *Abnormal Psychology*, 8, 9, 368, 405.

34. George Albee, Ph.D. (APA president, 1970), at the APA Annual Convention, San Francisco, 2001, cited in Bridget Murray, "Same Office, Different Aspirations," *Monitor on Psychology*, December 2001, 20.

35. "Practice Guidelines for the Assessment and Treatment of Patients with Suicidal Behaviors," *American Journal of Psychiatry* 160, no. 11 (November 2003): suppl. 10.

36. Andrew J. Weaver et al., "Is Religion Taboo in Psychology? A Systematic Analysis of Research on Religion in Seven Major American Psychological Journals, 1991–1994," *Journal of Psychology and Christianity* 17, no. 3 (1998): 220–32.

37. Peter L. Benson, Eugene C. Roehlkepartain, and Stacey P. Rude, "Spiritual Development in Childhood and Adolescence: Toward a Field of Inquiry," *Applied Developmental Science* 7, no. 3 (2003): 205–13.

38. K. A. Sherrill and D. B. Larson, "The Anti-Tenure Factor in Religious Research in Clinical Epidemiology and Aging," in *Religion in Aging and Health: Theoretical Foundations and Methodological Frontiers*, ed. J. S. Levin (Thousand Oaks, Calif.: Sage, 1994), 149–77.

39. John D. Gartner, "Antireligious Prejudice in Admissions to Doctoral Programs in Clinical Psychology," *Professional Psychology: Research and Practice* 17, no. 5 (1986): 473–75.

40. Richard E. Redding, "Sociopolitical Diversity in Psychology: The Case for Pluralism," *American Psychologist* 56, no. 3 (2001): 205–15.

41. I am including in this term other mental health professionals such as psychiatrists, social workers, MFTs, and so on.

42. The habits of individual practitioners may vary, but issues of faith and religious practice are given minimal consideration in patient education or intake forms on my campus. Likewise, a review of dozens of college health and counseling Web sites found no reference to issues of faith. Over ten years ago, the *Journal of American College Health* published a viewpoint by a pastoral counselor urging campus counselors to "recognize religious diversity in the student population and to include a discussion of spiritual values in the decision-making process." I do not see evidence that her call was heeded on my campus or elsewhere. (Florence Gelo, "Spirituality: A Vital Component of Health Counseling," *Journal of American College Health* 44 [July 1995]: 38–40.)

43. "What's in a Pill?" *Psychology Today*, May 2002, 4.

44. Richard Kadison and Theresa Foy DiGeronimo, *College of the Overwhelmed: The Campus Mental Health Crisis and What to Do About It* (San Francisco: Jossey-Bass, 2004).

45. J. Scott Young, Craig S. Cashwell, and Julia Shcherbakova, "The Moderating Relationship of Spirituality on Negative Life Events and Psychological Adjustment," *Counseling and Values* 45, no. 1 (October 2000): 49.

46. K. S. Masters et al., "Religious Life Styles and Mental Health: A Follow-up Study," *Counseling and Values* 35 (1991): 211–24.

47. Carl Sherman, "Personal Resilience Staves Off PTSD," *Clinical Psychology News* 34, no. 4 (April 2006): 1, 8.

48. www.spirituality.ucla.edu/spirituality/reports/final%20exec%20summary.pdf..

49. Andrew Newberg and Eugene D'Aquili, *Why God Won't Go Away* (New York: Random House, 2001).

50. Victor Frankl, *Man's Search for Meaning* (Boston: Beacon Press, 1959); M. Scott Peck, *The Road Less Traveled* (New York: Touchstone, 2003); Rick Warren, *The Purpose Driven Life* (Grand Rapids, Mich.: Inspirio, 2004).

Chapter IV. Saving Patient Brian

1. www.nyc.gov/html/doh/downloads/pdf/ah/surveillance2003_table3.1.pdf.

2. This way of tracking HIV was recently reported to have failed dismally. The *Los Angeles Times* stated, "The three year old reporting system for HIV has

become a bureaucratic morass.... Countless cases are believed to be lost in the system. As a result, health authorities ... cannot effectively monitor the epidemic or direct scarce dollars where they are most needed." This system was abandoned in August 2006. "HIV Tracking System May be Scrapped," *Los Angeles Times*, July 25, 2005.

3. http://www.cdc.gov/hiv/HERRG/considerations.htm.

4. Robert S. Janssen, "The Challenge of HIV Testing," guest editorial, *Clinical Psychiatry News*, vol. 32, no. 12 (December 2004): 7.

5. www.glma.org.

6. Robert Klitzman and Ronald Bayer, *Mortal Secrets: Truth and Lies in the Age of AIDS* (Baltimore, Md.: Johns Hopkins University Press, 2003).

7. L. P. Francis et al., "How Infectious Diseases Got Left Out—And What This Omission Might Have Meant for Bioethics," *Bioethics* 19, no. 4 (August 2005): 307.

8. Samuel A. Bozzette, "Routine Screening for HIV Infection—Timely and Cost-Effective," *New England Journal of Medicine*, 352, no. 6 (2005): 620.

9. A gripping firsthand account of these years is found in Stephen C. Joseph, *Dragon Within the Gates: The Once and Future AIDS Epidemic* (New York: Carroll & Graf, 1992).

10. Even if your partner died and was discovered on autopsy to be HIV-positive, you would not necessarily be informed, because this would violate the deceased's right to privacy.

11. Could things be changing? See Andrew Jacobs, "Gays

Debate Radical Steps to Curb Unsafe Sex," *New York Times*, February 15, 2005.

12. R. S. Gold and H. M. Aucote, " 'I'm Less at Risk Than Most Guys': Gay Men's Unrealistic Optimism about Becoming Infected with HIV," *International Journal of STDs and AIDS* 14, no. 1 (2003): 18–23.

CHAPTER V. SOPHIA'S MELTDOWN

1. I'm also assuming for the time being that Ken is not himself a member of a high-risk group—the recipient of a transfusion prior to April 1985, someone who has used intravenous drugs, or a man who has had sex with a man.

2. As of this writing, statistics on non-AIDS HIV infection by gender is not available for my state.

3. N. S. Padian, S. C. Shiboski, S. O. Glass, and E. Vittinghoff, "Heterosexual Transmission of Human Immunodeficiency Virus (HIV) in Northern California: Results from a Ten-Year Study," *American Journal of Epidemiology* 146, no 4: (1997) 350–57.

4. N. S. Padian, S. C. Shiboski, and N. P. Jewell, "Female-to-male Transmission of Human Immunodeficiency Virus," *Journal of the American Medical Association* 266, no. 12 (1991): 1664–67.

5. Joseph, *Dragon within the Gates*, 134–35.

6. Randy Shilts, *And the Band Played On: Politics, People, and the AIDS Epidemic* (New York: St. Martin's Press, 1987), 512–13. Some have tried to discredit this book, but I have reliable sources endorsing it, such as Bill Darrow, Ph.D., who wrote me in a per-

sonal communication (3/31/2006): "Believe in what Randy reported. For the most part, he was right on." Dr. Darrow could corroborate 90 percent of the book, he wrote, because he was there when it happened. He is currently a professor of public health at Florida International University. Previous to that, he served as chief, Behavioral and Prevention Research Branch, Division of STD/HIV Prevention, National Center for Prevention Services, Centers for Disease Control and Prevention (CDC).

7. This information was confirmed by Arthur Ammann, M.D., who cared for this woman and her children. At the time he was assistant professor of pediatric immunology at the University of California San Francisco Medical Center. He is currently president of Global Strategies for HIV Prevention.

8. Dr. Ammann stated that she had two, not three, children with HIV.

9. J. Reinisch, C. A. Hill, S. A. Sanders, and M. Ziemba-Davis, "High-Risk Sexual Behavior at a Midwestern University: A Confirmatory Survey," *Family Planning Perspectives* 27, no. 2 (1995): 79–82.

10. The classic text on this topic is Michael Fumento, *The Myth of Heterosexual AIDS* (New York: Basic Books, 1990).

11. www.merckmanual.com.

12. Luis Carlos Junqueira and Jose Carneiro, *Basic Histology: Text and Atlas*, 10th ed. (Columbus, Ohio: Lange Medical Books/McGraw-Hill, 2003).

13. Peter Greenhead et al., "Parameters of Human

Immunodeficiency Virus Infection of Human Cervical Tissue and Inhibition by Vaginal Virucides," *Journal of Virology*, June 2000, 5577–86.

14. B. Voeller and D. J. Anderson, letter to the editor, *Journal of the American Medical Association* 267 (1992): 1917–18, cited in S. Brody, *Sex at Risk: Lifetime Number of Partners, Frequency of Intercourse, and the Low AIDS Risk of Vaginal Intercourse* (Somerset, N.J.: Transaction Publishers, 1997), 216.

15. A. Moriyama, K. Shimoya, I. Ogata, T. Kimura, T. Nakamura, H. Wada, K. Ohashi, C. Azuma, F. Saji, and Y. Murata, "Secretory Leukocyte Protease Inhibitor (SLPI) Concentrations in Cervical Mucus of Women with Normal Menstrual Cycle," *Molecular Human Reproduction* 5 (1999): 656–61.

16. S. J. Robboy, M. Prade, and G. Cunha, "Normal Histology of the Uterus and Fallopian Tubes," in *Histology for Pathologists*, ed. S. S. Sternberg (North Holland, N.Y.: Raven Press, 1992), 881–92.

17. Peter Greenhead et al., "Parameters of Human Immunodeficiency Virus Infection of Human Cervical Tissue and Inhibition by Vaginal Virucides," *Journal of Virology*, June 2000, 5577–86.

18. M cells were actually first identified by Dr. Kenzaburo Kumagai of Osaka Tuberculosis Institute in 1922. Robert L. Owen, "Uptake and Transport of Intestinal Macromolecules and Microorganisms by M Cells in Peyer's Patches—A Personal and Historical Perspective," *Seminars in Immunology* 11(1999): 157–63.

19. A. D. O'Leary and E. C. Sweeney, "Lymphoglan-

dular Complexes of the Colon: Structure and Distribution," *Histopathology* 10 (1986): 267–83.

20. M. R. Neutra, N. J. Mantis, A. Frey, and P. J. Giannasca, "The Composition and Function of M Cell Apical Membranes: Implications for Microbial Pathogenesis," *Seminars in Immunology* 11 (1999): 171–81; Owen, "Uptake and Transport of Intestinal Macromolecules."

21. J. P. Kraehenbuhl and M. R. Neutra, *Physiological Reviews* 72 (1992) 853–79. This has been demonstrated in vitro but not in vivo.

22. Brody, *Sex at Risk*; Fumento, *Myth of Heterosexual AIDS*; and S. Chapman, "Dogma Disputed: Potential Endemic Heterosexual Transmission of Human Immunodeficiency Virus in Australia," *Australian Journal of Public Health* 16, no. 2 (1992): 128–41. For a cogent discussion of HIV/AIDS in Africa, and for scholarly critiques of the assumption that 90 percent of Africa's HIV is due to heterosexual transmission, see D. Gisselquist et al., "Let It Be Sexual: How Health Care Transmission of AIDS in Africa Was Ignored," *International Journal of STD & AIDS* 14 (2003): 148–61; letters to the editor in the same issue, 222–23; J. Glazov, "Symposium: The Radical Lies of AIDS," www.frontpagemag.com/Articles/Printable. asp?ID=18294; regarding the transmission of HIV via medical injections in poor countries, see "The Deadly Shot," *New York Times*, November 26, 2005; Cristian Apetrei et al., "Potential for HIV Transmission through Unsafe Injections," *AIDS* 20, no. 7

(2006): 1074–76 (letter); see also the Web site of John Potterat, www.geocities.com.

23. J. Potterat, D. Brewer, S. Muth, et al., "Mortality in a Long Term Open Cohort of Prostitute Women," *American Journal of Epidemiology* 159, no. 8 (2004): 778–85.

24. Fumento, *Myth of Heterosexual AIDS*, 78–79. Tertiary transmission, if it happens at all, is extremely rare.

25. N. Hearst and S. B. Hulley, "Preventing the Heterosexual Spread of AIDS: Are We Giving Our Patients the Best Advice?" *Journal of the American Medical Association* 259, no. 16 (April 22/29, 1988): 2428–32. The odds may be higher for a woman in sub-Saharan Africa or Thailand, but my concern is with my patient, and her risk.

26. www.nsc.org.

27. American College of Obstetricians and Gynecologists, *HIV Infection and Women*, patient education pamphlet (Washington, D.C.: American College of Obstetricians and Gynecologists, 1996).

28. www.cdc.gov/hiv/pubs/faq.

29. National Women's Health Network, Young Women's Editorial Team, "Young Women's Health," excerpted from *It's About Time!* (San Francisco: Girlsource, 2000). National Women's Health Network, in their "Lesbian Health" information packet, provides "The Story of a Lesbian with AIDS," from M. Arnold, *Caring for Ourselves: The Lesbian Health Book* (Seattle: Seal Press, 1997), 148–59. Contrary to what the title implies—that a woman was infected via

sex with a woman—the woman featured got AIDS via needle sticks during her years as a hospital lab technologist.

30. American Lung Association, www.lungusa.org.

31. A. R. Aro et al., "Fear of Acquired Immunodeficiency Syndrome and Fear of Other Illness in Suicide," *Acta Psychiatrica Scandinavica* 90 (1994): 65–69.

32. One-third were psychotic.

33. Amanda Bennett and Anita Sharpe, "Health Hazard: AIDS Fight Is Skewed by Federal Campaign Exaggerating Risks," *Wall Street Journal*, May 1, 1996.

34. *Life*, July 8, 1985; transcript of "Women Living with AIDS," episode of *Oprah Winfrey Show*, aired February 18, 1987, cited in Fumento, *The Myth of Heterosexual AIDS*.

35. Bennett and Sharpe, "Health Hazard."

36. G. Rotello, *Sexual Ecology: AIDS and the Destiny of Gay Men* (New York: Dutton/Penguin Books, 1997), p. 164.

37. D. Mertz, M. A. Shushinsky, and U. Schuklenk, "Women and AIDS: The Ethics of Exaggerated Harm," *Bioethics* 10, no. 2 (1996).

38. M. Lightfoot et al., "Risk Behaviors of Youths Living with HIV: Pre- and Post-HAART," *American Journal of Health Behavior* 29, no. 2 (2005): 162–71; Gold and Aucote, " 'I'm Less at Risk,' " 18–23.

39. Stephen Joseph, M.D., personal communication, December 1, 2005.

40. www.cdc.gov/hiv/topics/surveillance/basic.htm.

41. Bennett and Sharpe, "Health Hazard."

42. Shilts, *And the Band Played On*.

43.   Blurb on back cover of book.

44.   Randy Shilts, author's note, in *The Mayor of Castro Street: The Life and Times of Harvey Milk* (New York: St. Martin's Press, 1982).

45.   Shilts, *And the Band Played On*, 19.

46.   J. Warren and R. Paddock, "Randy Shilts, Chronicler of AIDS Epidemic, Dies at 42, Journalism: Author of 'And the Band Played On' Is Credited with Awakening Nation to the Health Crisis," *Los Angeles Times*, February 18, 1994.

Chapter VI. Kelly's Summer Vacation

1.   The availability of emergency contraception (known also as the "morning-after pill" and marketed under the name Plan B) has the potential to reduce unintended pregnancies and therefore prevent the trauma of abortion. On my campus, some practitioners at the student health center make sure sexually active women always have Plan B on hand, in case of future need. It makes some sense, as emergency contraception works best when taken within twenty-four hours, and, given that the center is closed on weekends and holidays, there may be delays in access. But I think it is naive to believe that having an abortifacient in their medicine cabinet won't affect the behavior of many women; being sexually active can expose them to other dangers.

2.   A sampling of their stories can be read on www.imnotsorry.com.

3.   www.plannedparenthood.com.

4.   Brenda Major et al., "Psychological Responses of

Women After First-Trimester Abortion," *Archives of General Psychiatry* 57, no. 8 (2000): 777–84. Other studies have found much higher rates of PTSD following induced abortion; see, for example, Vincent M. Rue et al., "Induced Abortion and Traumatic Stress: A Preliminary Comparison of American and Russian Women," *Medical Science Monitor* 10, no. 10 (2004): SR5–16.

5. They provide names of therapists and the number at the campus counseling center, but the student must make the initiative to schedule an appointment with someone they have never met, which may discourage some from seeking help.

6. I don't know if Kelly was given more information than I, but when I went to a Planned Parenthood clinic and asked to see all the material given to abortion patients, it had no mental health resources. Other branches of PP might have a different policy. I could not find information on postabortion counseling, support groups, or hotlines on the PP Web site or on its site for teens, teenwire.com.

7. Some therapists may ask, but the question is not a standard one.

8. Alan Guttmacher Institute, www.agi-usa.org: "From 1973 through 2002, more than 42 million legal abortions occurred."

9. www.afterabortion.com.

10. Anne C. Speckhard and Vincent M. Rue, "Postabortion Syndrome: An Emerging Public Health Concern," *Journal of Social Issues* 48, no. 3 (1992): 95–119.

11. Fifty-two percent, according to the Alan Guttemacher Institute.

12. Barbara J. Joachim, "The 'A' Word, *Journal of the American College Health Association* (July 1999): 47. Other articles acknowledging this issue on campus are: Yvonne M. DeCuir and M. Cynara Stites, "Decision-Making Model of Pregnancy Counseling," *Journal of American College Health* (April 1982): 244–47; Lawrence B. Siddall and Michael A. Cann, "Pregnancy on a University Campus," *Journal of American College Health Association* (February 1973): 247–51; Raymond S. Sanders, J. Mark Wagner, Georgine E. Thompson, "Counseling for Elective Abortion, *Journal of American College Health Association* 21 (June 1973): 446; Janet Urman and Sharon Meginnis, "The Process of Problem Pregnancy Counseling," *Journal of the American College Health Association* 28 (June 1980): 308–15; Stuart C. Tentoni, "A Theraputic Approach to Reduce Postabortion Grief in University Women," *Journal of American Health* (July 1995): 35–37.

13. In the journal, nothing since the 1999 "viewpoint" (issue 2 of volume 49 could not be reviewed); ACHA annual meetings of 2005 and 2006; in recent years, the availability of emergency contraception may have mitigated this problem.

14. www.healthyminds.org

15. Rebecca Vesely, "New Bay Area Hotline Offers Post-Abortion Counseling," www.womensnews.org, May 5, 2002.

16. There may be individual therapists who well under-

stand the potential trauma of an abortion, and help their patients as much as they can. I refer here to the stance taken by almost all medical, mental health, and women's organizations.

17. Constance Holden, "Koop Finds Abortion Evidence 'Inconclusive': Right-to-Lifers Fail to Get Hoped-for Evidence to Reverse *Roe v. Wade* When Supreme Court Reconsiders the Issue This Spring." *Science* 243 (February 1989): 730.

18. Susan Okie, "Abortion Report Koop Withheld Released on Hill," *Washington Post*, March 17, 1989.

19. Nancy Adler et al., "Psychological Factors in Abortion," *American Psychologist* 47, no. 10 (1992): 1194–1204.

20. "The Emotional Effects of Induced Abortion," www.plannedparenthood.com.

21. "Ask the Experts," www.teenwire.com.

22. Nada L. Stotland, "The Myth of the Abortion Trauma Syndrome," *Journal of the American Medical Association* 268 (1992): 2078–79.

23. http://clinton.senate.gov/~clinton/speeches/2005125A05.html/.

24. Wilbur J. Scott, "PTSD in DSM-III: A Case in the Politics of Diagnosis and Disease," *Social Problems* 37, no. 3 (1990): 294–310.

25. American Psychiatric Association, *Diagnostic and Statistical Manual of Mental Disorders*, 3d ed. (Washington, D.C.: American Psychiatric Association, 1980).

26. American Psychiatric Association, *Diagnostic and Statistical Manual of Mental Disorders*, 4th ed. (Washington, D.C.: American Psychiatric Association, 1994).

27. A. Young, *The Harmony of Illusions: Inventing Post-traumatic Stress Disorder* (Princeton, N.J.: Princeton University Press, 1995); Derek Summerfield, "The Invention of Post-Traumatic Stress Disorder and the Social Usefulness of a Psychiatric Category," *British Medical Journal* (January 13, 2001): 95–98.

28. Claudia Avina and William O'Donohue, "Sexual Harassment and PTSD: Is Sexual Harassment Diagnosable Trauma?" *Journal of Traumatic Stress* 15, no. 1 (February 2002): 69–75; Sandra Gold, "Post-Traumatic Stress Disorder May Follow Childbirth," *British Medical Journal* 313 (September 1996): 774.

29. This site represents only one resource for women and men distressed following an abortion. There are many other organizations providing similar services, but they are sectarian and vigorously pro-life, like SafeHavenMinistries.com or RachelsVineyard.org, which has weekend retreats in forty-three states and twelve countries. These retreats for men and women are "an opportunity to deeply enter the grieving process and identify all the ways your abortion may have affected you."

30. Anne Nordal Broen et al., "The Course of Mental Health after Miscarriage and Induced Abortion: A Longitudinal, Five-Year Follow-up Study," *BMC Medicine* 3 (2005): 18; Brenda Major, "Beyond Choice: Myths and Facts about Adjustment to Abortion," in *1997 Wellness Lectures*, California Wellness Foundation and the University of California; P. G. Ney and A. R. Wickett, "Mental Health and Abortion: Review and Analysis," *Psychiatric Journal of the Univer-*

sity of Ottawa 14, no. 4 (1989): 506–16; John M. Thorp, Katherine E. Hartmann, and Elizabeth Shadigian, "Long-Term Physical and Psychological Health Consequences of Induced Abortion: Review of the Evidence," *Obstetrical and Gynecological Survey* 58, no. 1 (2002): 67–79; Zoe Bradshaw and Pauline Slade, "The Effects of Induced Abortion on Emotional Experiences and Relationships: A Critical Review of the Literature," *Clinical Psychology Review* 23, no. 7 (2003): 929–58; and others.

31. Men's reactions have been studied, but generally only in the context of how they impact the woman's response.

32. Arthur B. Shostak and Gary McLouth, *Men and Abortion: Lessons, Losses, and Love* (New York: Praeger, 1984).

33. The authors report that 50 percent of men do not accompany their partners, so these results are skewed. When they gathered data from eighteen men who had been absent, they found lower rates of agreement with the abortion, and somewhat higher opposition to abortion per se. About these "men waiting elsewhere" ("up to 600,000 men a year") they conclude, "We believe many suffer far more ill effects than anyone now suspects" (139).

34. Arthur B. Shostak, "Motivations of Abortion Clinic Waiting Room Males: 'Bottled-Up Roles and Unmet Needs,' " in *Changing Men: New Directions in Research on Men and Masculinity*, ed. Michael Kimmel (Thousand Oaks, Calif.: Sage, 1987), 193.

35. Shostak and Gary McLouth, *Men and Abortion*, 64.

36. B. Major et al., "Male Partners' Appraisals of Undesired Pregnancy and Abortion: Implications for Women's Adjustment to Abortion," *Journal of Applied Social Psychology* vol. 22, no. 8 (1992): 610–11.

37. R. A. Gordon and C. Kilpatrick, "A Program of Group Counseling for Men Who Accompany Women Seeking Legal Abortions," *Community Mental Health Journal* 13 (1977): 291–95; P. Lauzon et al., "Emotional Distress among Couples Involved in First-Trimester Induced Abortions," *Canadian Family Physician* 47 (February 2001): 249; J. S. Wallerstein, P. Kurtz, and Marion Bar-Din, "Psychosocial Sequelae of Therapeutic Abortion in Young Unmarried Women," *Archives of General Psychiatry* 27, no. 8 (1972): 828–32; and A. A. Rothstein, "Men's Reactions to Their Partners' Elective Abortions," *American Journal of Obstetrics and Gynecology* 128, no. 8 (1977): 831–37.

38. George Skelton, "Many in Survey Who Had Abortion Cite Guilt Feelings," *Los Angeles Times*, March 19, 1989; Rebecca Vesely, "New Bay Area Hotline Offers Post-Abortion Counseling," *Womensnews*, May 5, 2002.

39. Arthur Shostak, "No, I am NOT a 'Rock': On Abortion and Waiting Room Men," *SWS Network News: The Newsletter of Sociologists for Women in Society*, December 2003.

40. To say nothing of "victims of oppression": sexism, racism, ageism, heterosexism, able-ism.

41. Unwanted parenthood and adoption may also bring emotional problems to everyone involved.

42. Planned Parenthood, "How Is a D&C Performed?" www.plannedparenthood.com.

43. Marianne Wan-Hey Chow, "Coping with Silence: Comparative Analysis on Post-abortion Grief in Japan and the United States" (honors thesis, Department of International Relations, Tufts University, 2003). Found on www.pregnantpause.org/aborted/japcope.pdf.

44. William LaFleur, *Liquid Life* (Princeton, N.J.: Princeton University Press, 1992), 24.

45. Chow, "Coping with Silence," 21. Translation by the author.

46. Daphne de Marneffe, *Maternal Desire: On Children, Love, and the Inner Life* (Little, Brown, 2004), 237–38.

CHAPTER VII. DELIA'S DREAM

1. Paul Beeson et al, eds., *Cecil Textbook of Medicine*, 15th ed. (Philadelphia: W. B. Saunders, 1979), 332–35.

2. David M. Ojcius et al., "Can Chlamydia Be Stopped?" *Scientific American*, May 2005, 72–79.

3. Diaa M. El-Mowafi and M. Diamond, "Fallopian Tubes," in Ernst Knobil and Jimmy Neill, eds., *Encyclopedia of Reproduction* (San Diego, Calif.: Academic Press, 1998), 2:150–52.

4. Steven S. Witkin, personal communication, May 14, 2005.

5. D. Patton et al., "Significant Reduction in the Macaque Model of Chlamydial Pelvic Inflammatory Disease with Azithromycin Treatment," *Journal of Infectious Diseases* 192 (July 2005): 129–35.

6. Jolande A. Land et al., "Chlamydia Trachomatis in Subfertile Women Undergoing Uterine Instrumentation," *Human Reproduction* 17, no. 3 (March 2002): p. 525.

7. Joseph Debattista et al., "Immunopathogenesis of *Chlamydia trachomis* Infections in Women," *Fertility and Sterility* 79, no. 6 (June 2003): 1273–87.

8. S. Faro and D. E. Soper, eds., *Infectious Diseases in Women* (Philadelphia: W. B. Saunders, 2000), 261–62.

9. D. L. Sipkin, A. Gillam, and L. B. Grady, "Risk Factors for Chlamydia Trachomatis Infection in a California Collegiate Population," *Journal of American College Health* 52, no. 2 (2003): 65–71.

10. American College Health Association, National College Health Assessment, Spring 2004 Reference Group Data Report (abridged), *Journal of American College Health* 54, no. 4 (2006): p. 207.

11. Stuart N. Seidman and Sevgi Okten Aral, "Behavioral Aspects of Pelvic Inflammatory Disease," in *Pelvic Inflammatory Disease*, ed. Daniel Landers and Richard Sweet (New York: Springer, 1997), 181.

12. Joan M. Chow and Julius Schachter, "Long-term Sequelae of Pelvic Inflammatory Disease: Tubal Factor Infertility, Ectopic Pregnancy, and Chronic Pelvic Pain," in Landers, ed., *Pelvic Inflammatory Disease*, 161–62; Steven S. Witkin et al., "Unsuspected *Chlamydia trachomatis* Infection and In Vitro Fertilization Outcome," *American Journal of Obstetrics and Gynecology* 171, no. 5 (1994): 1213; Virginia Morell, "Attacking the Causes of 'Silent Infertility,'" *Science* 269, no. 5225 (August 11, 1995): 775.

13. A. Neuer et al., "Heat Shock Protein Expression during Gametogenesis and Embryogenesis," *Infectious Diseases in Obstetrics and Gynecology* 7 (1999): 10–16; A. Neuer et al., "Humoral Immune Response to Membrane Components of *Chlamydia trachomatis* and Expression of Human 60 kDa Heat Shock Protein in Follicular Fluid of In-vitro Fertilization Patients," *Human Reproduction* 12, no. 5 (1997): 925.

14. Patton et al., "Significant Reduction in the Macaque Model."

15. Jeffrey F. Peipert, "Genital Chlamydia Infections," *New England Journal of Medicine* 349, no. 25 (December 2003): 2427–28.

16. www.fda.gov/fdac/features/1999/499_std.html.

17. John J. Potterat, "Active Detection of Men with Asymptomatic Chlamydial or Gonorrheal Urethritis" (letter), *International Journal of STD & AIDS* 16 (June 2005): 458.

18. E. S. Berg, G. Anestad, H. Hoi, G. Storvold, and K. Skaug, "False Negative Results of a Ligase Chain Reaction Assay to Detect Chlamydia trachomatis Due to Inhibitors in Urine," *European Journal of Clinical Microbiology and Infectious Disease* 16, no. 10 (October 1997): 727–31.

19. Richard Keeling, "The College Health Opportunity," editorial, *Journal of American College Health* 49, no. 6 (May 2001): 249.

20. Maryann Leslie and Richard St. Pierre, "Osteoporosis: Implications for Risk Reduction in the College Setting," *Journal of American College Health* 48 (September 1999).

21. Leon Speroff, R. H. Glass, and N. G. Kase, *Clinical Gynecologic Endocrinology and Infertility*, 2nd ed. (Baltimore, Md. Williams & Wilkins, 1978), 322.

Chapter VIII. Amanda's Thirty-ninth Birthday

1. "If you are a healthy 30-year-old woman, you have about a 20% chance per month to get pregnant. By age 40, however, your chance is only about 5% per month." From American Society for Reproductive Medicine, *Age and Fertility, a Guide for Patients* (Birmingham, Ala.: American Society for Reproductive Medicine, 2003), 3.

2. American Society for Reproductive Medicine, *Age and Fertility, a Guide for Patients* (Birmingham, Ala.: American Society for Reproductive Medicine, 2003); Linda Heffner, Advanced "Maternal Age—How Old Is Too Old?" *New England Journal of Medicine* 351 (November 2004): 1; Robert K. Creasy and Robert Resnick, eds., *Maternal Fetal Medicine: Practice and Principles* (Philadelphia: W. B. Saunders, 1994), 71.

3. American Society for Reproductive Medicine, American Society for Reproductive Medicine Guide for Patients, *Infertility: An Overview* (Birmingham, Ala.: American Society for Reproductive Medicine, 2003), 4.

4. Diana Kapp, "Getting Off the Stick," *Elle*, July 2004, 112.

5. "Ice, Ice Baby," *Elle*, April 2004 (from www.extendfertility.com).

6. ASRM Guide for Patients, *Ovulation Drugs* (Birmingham, Ala.: American Society for Reproductive Medicine, 2000), 9.

7. American Society for Reproductive Medicine, *Ovulation Drugs*, 15.

8. Ronald T. Burkman et al., "Infertility Drugs and Risk of Breast Cancer: Findings from the National Institute of Child Health and Human Development Women's Contraceptive and Reproductive Experiences Study," *Fertility and Sterility* 79, no. 4 (April 2003): 844–51; Louise A. Brinton et al., "Ovulation Induction and Cancer Risk," *Fertility and Sterility* 83, no. 2 (February 2005): 261–74; and Asher Shushan and Neri Laufer, "Fertility Drugs and Ovarian Cancer: What Are the Practical Implications of the Ongoing Debate?" *Fertility and Sterility* 74, no. 1 (July 2000): 8–9.

9. A. D. Domar et al., "The Psychological Impact of Infertility: A Comparison with Patients with Other Medical Conditions," *Journal of Psychosomatic Obstetrics and Gynecology* 14 suppl. (1993): 45–52.

10. Björn J. Oddens et al, "Psychosocial Experiences in Women Facing Fertility Problems—A Comparative Survey," *Human Reproduction* 14, no. 1 (1999): 255–61.

11. Claudia Kalb, "Should You Have Your Baby Now?" *Newsweek*, August 13, 2001, 40.

12. Sylvia Ann Hewlett, *Creating a Life: Professional Women and the Quest for Children* (New York: Hyperion, 2002), 219.

13. Ibid., 218.

14. Ibid., 205.

15. Ibid., 89.

16. Kalb, "Should You Have Your Baby."

17. Hewlett, *Creating a Life*, 217.

18. *Yahoo! News*, January 16, 2005.

19. Zev Rosenwaks, "We Still Can't Stop the Biological Clock," *New York Times*, June 24, 2000.

20. Rick Weiss, "Infertility Campaign Can't Get Ad Space," *Washington Post*, August 28, 2002.

21. Sean Tipton, American Society for Reproductive Medicine director of public affairs, personal communication, April 6, 2005.

22. www.extendfertility.com.

23. From www.extendfertility.com.

24. www.extendfertility.com.

25. Kate Johnson, "Oocyte Freezing: Insurance or False Security?" *Clinical Psychiatry News*, February 2005, 76. Concerning egg freezing, Dr. Zev Rosenwaks, director of the Center for Reproductive Medicine and Infertility at Weill Medical College of Cornell University, said: "I feel very strongly that this technology is absolutely not ready for prime time. My biggest concern is the issue of false security." Quoted in "Ice, Ice Baby," *Elle*, April 2004, and found on extendfertility.com. A spokeswoman for the Society for Assisted Reproductive Technology said, "It's something that isn't really ready to be offered commercially, because the success rates for it still aren't very good. It's still under development, and a lot of work is still needed." Quoted in Joan Morris, "Banking on Science for Future Fertility," *Contra Costa Times*, April 18, 2006.

26. www.extendfertility.com, press release, June 2, 2004.

27. Erik H. Erikson, *Identity: Youth in Crisis* (New York: W. W. Norton, 1968), 138.

28. George E. Vaillant, *Aging Well: Surprising Guideposts to a Happier Life from the Landmark Harvard Study of Adult Development* (New York: Little, Brown, 2002), 113.

29. Calvin A. Colarusso, *Fulfillment in Adulthood: Paths to the Pinnacle of Life* (New York: Plenum Press, 1994).

30. D. A. Luzzo, ed., *Career Counseling of College Students* (Washington, D.C.: American Psychological Association, 2000), 44.

31. Ibid., 253–65.

32. Ibid., 255.

33. Ibid., 261.

34. Ibid., 263.

35. Ibid., 264.

36. Perhaps individual health providers address the issue of fertility, but I see no evidence of it—no handouts, posters, official policy statements, etc.

37. Ted W. Grace, "Health Problems of College Students," *Journal of American College Health* 45, no. 6 (May 1997): 244.

38. Gail Kramer, "Fertility Awareness: The University of California/Berkeley Experience," *Journal of American College Health* 31 (February 1983): 166–67.

39. www.aauw.org.

40. www.plannedparenthood.org.

41. Politically correct, of course.

42. Hewlett, *Creating a Life*, 47.

43. Ibid., 33, 86, 2–3.

44. Ibid., 38–40.

45. Ibid., 98–99.

46. Ibid., 304.

47. Ibid., 201.

48. "Mom, 66: 'We Should Not Count on Miracles,'" abcnews.go.com, April 14, 2005.

CONCLUSION

1. Richard Kadison and Theresa Foy DiGeronimo, *College of the Overwhelmed: The Campus Mental Health Crisis and What to Do About It* (San Francisco: Jossey-Bass, 2004).

2. Only the pain of women, however.

3. Sherry A. Benton et al., "Changes in Counseling Center Client Problems across 13 Years," *Professional Psychology: Research and Practice* 34, no. 1 (2003): 66–72; Lisa M. Sodders, "College Hard on Mental Health," *Los Angeles Daily News*, August 12, 2002: "'Most come in saying they're lonely and depressed, often over a failed romance,' said Bradford D. King, director of USC's student counseling services"; Linda J. Sax, "Health Trends among College Freshmen," *Journal of American College Health* 45, no. 6 (1997): 252–62: "Upon entering college, women consistently report more depression and stress than men do, a gender difference that increases during the 4 years of college."

4. Scott Dotterer and I. Renee Axiotis, "Sex-Tac-Toe," *Journal of American College Health* 43 (1994): 137–39.

5. Joanna Hayden, "The Condom Race," *Journal of American College Health* 42, no. 3 (1993): 133.

6. From a workshop at the 2005 meeting of the American College Health Association, "Same Models/ Different Programs: Using the Ecological Model and the Standards of Practice for Health Promotion in Higher Education to Address HIV Risk in College Students."

7. This could be accomplished with a patient education pamphlet.

8. Even if we ask, some will not be ready to tell, but at least it opens a door.

9. American College Health Association, *Woman to Woman: Three Steps to Health for Lesbian, Bisexual, or Any Women Who Have Sex with Women* and *Man to Man: Three Steps to Health for Gay, Bisexual, or Any Men Who Have Sex with Men* (Baltimore, Md.: American College Health Association, 2003); American College Health Association, *Safer Sex* and *Making Sex Safer* (Baltimore, Md.: American College Health Association, 2002).

10. Marianne J. Legato, ed., *Principles of Gender-Specific Medicine* (San Diego, Calif.: Elsevier, 2004).

11. John Colapinto, *As Nature Made Him: The Boy Who Was Raised as a Girl* (New York: HarperCollins, 2000).

12. Nancy Adler et al. "Psychological Factors in Abortion," *American Psychologist* 47, no. 10 (1992): 1197.

13. "The Homosexual Movement: A Response by the Ramsey Colloquium," *First Things* 41 (March 1994): 15–21.

INDEX